Getting paid to
DRINK *and*
GAMBLE

Jeff Collerson joined the late Sir Frank Packer's *Daily* and *Sunday Telegraphs* in 1962, after leaving Enmore Boys' High School armed with his Leaving Certificate, the equivalent of today's HSC.

From the age of eight, when he began typing his own newspapers on a portable typewriter, Collerson had never wanted to be anything but a journalist. In 1968 he was 'poached' by legendary racing columnist Pat Farrell to become the greyhounds writer on Rupert Murdoch's *Daily Mirror*. When Murdoch later bought the *Daily Telegraph*, Collerson became the paper's greyhound expert and by 1988 had added the paper's wine column and reviews to his duties. Midway through 2005 he was appointed as one of the *Tele*'s two restaurant reviewers, so this book could justifiably be re-titled *Getting Paid to Drink, Gamble and Eat*. Collerson is the host of one of radio's longest running sport programs, 'Going Greyhounds', heard Thursday mornings on 2KY. He has owned and trained racing pigeons and greyhounds and led separate tours to the USA and Europe. His hobbies are listening to soul and blues music, following Manly-Warringah rugby league team and betting on the dogs.

Born in 1945 in the Sydney northern beaches suburb of Harbord, Collerson now lives in north-west Sydney with wife Catherine and children Nicolas, Dion, Sophie and Nathalie.

Getting paid to DRINK and GAMBLE

JEFF 'PIGEON' COLLERSON

Yarns and tales from *The Daily Telegraph's* racing and wine journalist

ABC
Books

Published by ABC Books for the
AUSTRALIAN BROADCASTING CORPORATION
GPO BOX 9994 Sydney NSW 2001

First published 2005

National Library of Australia
Cataloguing in Publication entry
Collerson, Jeff.
    Getting paid to drink and gamble.

    ISBN 0 7333 1730 8.

    1. Greyhound racing – Australia - Anecdotes. 2. Gambling –
    Australia – Anecdotes. 3. Drinking of alcoholic beverages –
    Anecdotes. I. Australian Broadcasting Corporation.

798.850994

Cover and internal design by Darian Causby/Highway 51 and Luke Causby/Bluecork
Typeset in 11/14 Sabon by Asset Typesetting Pty Ltd, Moruya
Printed in Australia by Griffin Press, South Australia

5 4 3 2 1

Dedication

When my wife Catherine and I were about to be married I warned her I was a gambler and while there would probably be bad times mixed with the good she should not try to change me. She didn't and while, thanks to backing more fast dogs than slow ones, the good times have outnumbered the bad, she has stuck to me like mud to a blanket.

For her sins she has had listen to the anecdotes in this book hundreds of times at lunches, dinners and gatherings, all the while feigning stoically that they were all brand new to her.

For all that, Catherine, 'ma petite grenouille' (my little frog), this book is dedicated to you.

Acknowledgements

To Barossa winemaker Peter Lehmann and his wife Margaret, who first encouraged me to put pen to paper and write this book.

To Richard Zammit, with whom I've shared hundreds of long lunches, and Noel Christensen, for encouraging me to continue when I felt like chucking it in.

To the late Murray Tyrrell. The legendary winemaker had asked me to write his biography but sadly died before we had the chance to do it. I think he would approve of this.

To all those 'salt-of-the-earth' characters in the racing and wine industries who have provided the inspiration and substance for is assortment of yarns.

And to my son Dion, who helped me, someone who is hard pressed logging on to a computer, put everything together.

CONTENTS

1

The Pitfalls of Being a Tipster

They say that tipping — not the restaurant but the racetrack kind — is the odds to a kicking. Apart from when it is part of your job, if the selection wins there is seldom a reward but if it loses it can create animosity, even to the extent of losing a friend. I've tipped to a couple of very high profile people, and neither exercise turned out well.

In the early 1960s, as a cadet journalist working on the old Consolidated Press-owned *Daily Telegraph*, one of my tasks was to sift through the Saturday night dog fields in order to give my tips to Kerry Packer. In those days Kerry's father Sir Frank was the managing director of Consolidated Press and Kerry was then, as now, an enthusiastic punter.

I used to work at the horse races during the day but had to be back at my desk between 6 and 6.30 pm to await Kerry's phone call before leaving for the dogs at Harold or Wentworth Parks. I had a pretty good record for several months but it used to bug me that there was seldom a thankyou for my reasonably accurate race forecasting.

My involvement with Kerry came to an end one night when I declared a dog called The Shoe, who was a Harold Park specialist, a certainty in a race there. The Shoe got beaten, as they all do sooner or later, and Kerry poked his head into the sporting room door 48 hours later to give me a blast. In hindsight it was almost certainly part of Kerry's quirky sense of humour, as while berating me he said with a broad grin that he didn't know how I held a job as the dog tipster for his dad's paper.

I didn't see the joke in the pay, which was delivered in front of my immediate boss, turf editor Keith Robbins. After all, I had received no praise for tipping winners yet was getting a roast over one loser. So I replied in kind, giving Kerry a return spray. Luckily for me, Keith backed me up, cheekily telling Kerry that maybe The Shoe was only my second string tip. 'Haven't you been slinging for the winners?' a cocky Keith asked of the boss's son. (A 'sling' is a financial reward.) 'No, I thought that the fact that my father is the managing director of this company would cut a bit of ice,' Kerry replied. I jumped in with: 'It doesn't cut any ice with me.' With that, Kerry turned and left, and never called me again. But at least I kept my job.

Many years later, when I was working for News Limited on the *Daily Mirror*, world boxing champion Jeff Fenech and his trainer Johnnie Lewis turned up one night at Harold Park dogs in search of tips. My mate Bill 'Bluegum' Mordey, who had been the boxing editor of the *Daily Mirror*, was now a fight promoter and handled the Fenech fights. 'Bill Mordey said you could mark our books,' said Jeff, meaning give them some tips.

I obliged and, as fate would have it, tipped a stack of winners. Naturally Jeff was back at the track for the next race meeting, 48 hours later, probably wondering how long this had being going on. Like all punters and tipsters, my luck runs in cycles, and Jeff happened to catch me on a winning streak.

Jeff was a generous bloke and wanted to send me a case of Chivas Regal whisky as a thankyou, but I declined, not through taking the high moral ground but because of my long friendship with Bill Mordey. Jeff began attending the dogs regularly and was terrific with kids, as I never once saw him refuse to stop for a chat or to sign an autograph. But it wasn't long before I was glad I had said no to the Gordon & Gotch (Scotch). The tips started getting beaten, and one night at Harold Park I found Jeff in the betting ring an hour before the first race.

He had arrived early because he owed some money to a bookie named Con Kafataris, a result, Jeff informed me, of my recent dud tips. Here I was thinking Jeff was a $20 punter, so I was mortified to hear I had cost him a substantial amount of cash. 'Listen, mate,' I told him, 'if I was a genius I wouldn't be getting up at six in the morning and working for Rupert Murdoch.' Jeff said not to worry about it, but then asked me for my selections for that night. I explained I liked only two dogs, one in the first and the other in the second race. 'Great,' said Jeff. 'I have to be at the gym at 8.30 but I'll be able to have a couple of bets before I leave.' The first dog missed a place but the second, carrying the black rug, number seven, raced away with a big lead at good odds. But in the last bound another greyhound got up to beat it in a photo finish.

From a couple of rows behind me in the press section, where Jeff used to sit, my colleagues and I heard a resounding 'FUCK!!!' followed by a crash. The crash turned out to be Jeff punching the wooden table in front of him, and it was still reverberating as he vaulted over a couple of rows to reach me. My mates turned out to be as solid as Aeroplane Jelly and evaporated while Jeff dragged me out of my seat. I thought I was about to cop a hammering but he immediately laughed and gave me a playful slap across the face. 'I was only mucking around, mate, it's a joke,' he said. It could well have been too, but I was awfully close to needing a change of underwear.

After that experience I sacked myself as Jeff's greyhound tipster. A couple of other punters who listened to my dog tips gave me less angst. One was the late David McNicoll, who was editor-in-chief of Consolidated Press when I worked for the *Daily Telegraph*. The other was Will Ryan, a Sydney hotelier who also owned a winery in the Hunter Valley.

It was David who gave me the nickname Pigeon, which has stuck to this day. When I started work at the *Tele*, straight from Enmore Boys' High School in 1962, I had racing pigeons. In fact while I was still a copy boy I did a feature story, at David's suggestion, on the history of that hobby. I had always been a big sports fan and as a kid was a regular spectator at the Monday night fights at the old Sydney Stadium, Rushcutters Bay, the Thursday night wrestling at Leichhardt Stadium, and at the horse races. The only reason I hadn't been to the dogs or trots was that in those days kids under 18 were not permitted to attend those sports. Horse racing was fine, but in a bizarre situation, the powers that be of the 1950s decided the dogs and trots were somehow more likely than the horses to lead young people astray.

Fortunately that situation had changed by the time I became a cadet journalist in the *Daily Telegraph* sporting department. My initial duties included covering minor boxing bouts and rugby league matches, as well as doing race results. I also wrote horse form (known as comment) and tipped for the horses under the noms-de-plume Madame X and Horscope. *The Telegraph* greyhound writer at the time was Mike Gibson, now well known in Sydney radio and television. Mike was about to switch from the dogs to become the *Telegraph*'s chief rugby league writer, replacing veteran footy scribe George Crawford. That meant a new greyhound writer had to be found and, because this entailed working every Saturday night, none of the married racing writers wanted the task. Because I was the only single member on the racing staff, I was told I was to replace Gibbo.

And that's how I became David McNicoll's dog tipster. Before I headed out to the track — just after giving Kerry Packer my selections over the phone — I had to pop into David's office to collect his night's punting bank. After each race I would phone through the results for the *Sunday Telegraph*, perhaps do a story, and then call David to advise him of the state of his punting finances. Sometimes he would have had a whisper about a dog, but mostly he took my tips.

At the end of the night, if he had any money left, I had to jump on a bus at Glebe and return to the *Telegraph* offices on the corner of Castlereagh and Park streets. This time I would knock on the boardroom door, where invariably I would find David, *SundayTelegraph* editor Johnny Moyes, *Daily Telegraph* editor

King Watson, and sometimes Alan Barnes, one of the *Tele*'s crack reporters, sharing a bottle of Scotch. Occasionally David would give me a couple of quid as a reward for my tips, which wasn't bad considering I was earning less than a tenner a week.

Newspapers were, like a lot of industries, far different then from how they are now. I can't imagine being sent to the track these days with money to bet on behalf of Rupert or Lachlan Murdoch, although I have shared ownership of a greyhound with John Hartigan, News Limited's CEO. Harto and I, along with Kevin Scanlon, at the time national sales manager of De Bortoli Wines, *Daily Tele* sports editor Tim Mullins and sporting columnist Ray Kershler, were partners in a dog called Brother Eddie. The greyhound, which we bought for only $3000, was trained by a knockabout bloke named Dick Riley and won a race at Wentworth Park in September 1997, as well as the final of the Maitland Derby on 26 June 1996. We had heaps of fun with Brother Eddie but mostly spent his race earnings on slap-up meals at posh restaurants like Tetsuya's.

I had known Tetsuya Wakuda, now a world-famous chef, from his early days in Sydney and we had become good mates. At one luncheon, John Hartigan, Piers Akerman, the *Daily Telegraph* columnist, and Col Allen, then *Daily Telegraph* editor and now boss of the *New York Post*, were joined late in the day by Lachlan Murdoch. Lachlan had not been able to get away for the full lunch, but when he arrived around 3 pm I asked Tetsuya to send him up a sample plate of small entree selections and some dessert.

Around 4.30 news came through to Lachlan that Frank Sinatra had died. Lachlan instructed Col Allen to come up with a snappy headline for the following day's *Telegraph,* and yours truly, by this late hour with a couple of bottles of red under my belt, suggested: 'Old Blue Eyes Is Dead'. Lachlan didn't seem impressed so I decided to button up in case I talked my way out of a job.

The postscript to that lunch put me under some pressure, though. Lachlan, who I found to be modest, polite and interesting, liked Tetsuya's so much he wanted to return a week later. This time he wanted to take his wife Sarah O'Hare along. Problem was the place was, as always, booked out several weeks in advance. Col Allen came around to see me at my desk, where I was punching out the Bulli dog form. 'We have a problem, mate,' Col said. 'My secretary and Lachlan's secretary have phoned Tetsuya's and the best the manager there can do is put Lachlan and Sarah on a wait list. Can you do anything?' I phoned Tetsuya direct and the affable Tet, whose restaurant in those days was a tiny place in Darling Street, Rozelle, obliged, slipping in an extra table for the boss and his missus.

I often wonder if I got the brownie points from Lachlan or whether Col claimed the credit for himself. Good luck to him if he did. Peter Forrestal, then editor of the *Australian Gourmet Traveller Wine* magazine, loved that story. Forry used to relate the tale, saying: 'Lachlan Murdoch's secretary couldn't get him in to Tetsuya's but the *Telegraph*'s dog man did!'

Incidentally, my racing contacts once enabled me to organise a couple of Melbourne Cup members' stand tickets for Kevin Scanlon, the De Bortoli Wines boss. Kevin was going to Melbourne but had not had any luck securing a couple of sought-after members' stand briefs for the big race. So he asked if I could help. I called an old mate, Bob Charley, who was then chairman of the Australian Jockey Club. Bob pointed out that the Victorian Racing Club had cut back on tickets and that while Kevin and his wife were welcome to join him and his committee at Randwick on Cup day, tickets to Flemington were impossible to secure. But I found a way.

Another racing contact assured me he obtained forged tickets each year, and that they would cost just $50 apiece. I was a bit concerned, envisioning the trump of a major wine company getting arrested for being in possession of fake members' stand passes. But my contact assured me the tickets were impossible to detect and that in previous years he had provided them for knights of the realm. I got the tickets, but when I handed them over I did not tell Kevin they were fakes. He later told me he and his wife had a ball and were so close to the action they could have almost led the winning horse back to scale.

David McNicoll was a revelation. He had some great anecdotes, but none better than one concerning him I heard from a colleague. It apparently occurred when Sir Frank Packer sent David off to London on an important assignment. David arrived mid-winter, and being a man of impeccable style he immediately purchased a Burberry overcoat, just about the swankiest available in the Old Dart. When he returned, he submitted his swindle sheet to Sir Frank, who had a reputation for being tough on expenses.

Sir Frank called David into his office and agreed to pay a range of costs, such as taxi fare from Heathrow to the London CBD and so forth. But he baulked at a McNicoll item which read: 'Overcoat, £100'. When queried about this the unflappable McNicoll replied that because we live in a temperate climate he did not possess an overcoat and thought it reasonable that he purchase one for the duration of his working trip.

Sir Frank was equally unruffled, asking why it was necessary to spend £100 on the garment. 'Sir Frank, I was representing Consolidated Press at important functions, and I thought you would surely want me to look the part,' was David's explanation. To which Sir Frank retorted: 'Okay, that's fair enough. I'll tell you what to do. Bring the office overcoat in tomorrow and I'll hang it on that hook on my wall to lend to the next reporter I send to Europe.'

Will Ryan turned up at Wentworth Park dogs one night in 2003 and, having met me at a wine function, sought me out for some tips. I assumed he was only a small punter out for a night of entertainment, but noticed him beaming after I managed to snare a few good-priced winners. It was then that Mark Merlino, one of the Wenty bookies and a good friend, called me over to his stand. 'Are you tipping to that bloke over there?' he asked, gesturing towards Ryan. 'Yes,' I replied. 'Someone said you were seen talking to him. He has absolutely destroyed Jeff Pendlebury [another bookie] tonight and in turn has ruined everything for me and John Stollery.'

Will was a regular client of bookmaker Jeff Pendlebury at the horses, and began betting with him at the dogs on my tips. Because Will was betting so big, and the pools at the dogs are so much smaller than at the horses, Pendlebury laid off part of each of his bets with Merlino and Stollery, also a pal of mine. The mail was that Will won a healthy five-figure sum on the night, an amount practically unheard of at the dogs. Naturally he was back for the next few meetings, believing he had discovered a genius in yours truly, but alas, the wheels fell off and I could barely find him a winner.

I'll talk more about Bill Mordey in another chapter, but the boxing/rugby league-journo-turned-fight promoter thought he too had found a talented tipster when we attended a horse race meeting at Auteuil, France, in 1972. Mordey was there covering the rugby league World Cup for the *Daily Mirror*, while E.E. (Ernie) Christensen was doing likewise for the *Mirror*'s afternoon newspaper rival, the *Sun*. I was there too, thanks to backing a few winners, and enjoying a holiday following the fortunes of the Aussie team.

On a free day the three of us headed off to Auteuil, where the entire program was made up of steeplechase races. Ernie and I were only out for a day of fun, but Bluegum Mordey never attended a race meeting on that basis. It wouldn't matter where in the world he was — the Tijuana cockfights included — he had to bet like there was no tomorrow. As we approached the track, I asked Mordey how he was going to work out which horses to back.

'Simple, Pigeon, we'll follow the money like we do in Australia,' was his curt reply. When I pointed out this would be difficult because there were no bookmakers in France, he decided we should seek out tips from the racetrack press room. Again there was a problem. Walk into a press room at a race, dog or trotting track in Australia and you'll find the occupants will have varying degrees of skill at selecting winners.

'How will we know who to ask?' I wondered aloud as we knocked on the press room door at Auteuil. Seated around a table playing cards were half a dozen desperado-type characters, obviously the cream of the French racing press. Because Mordey had been complaining long and loud about the price of food from the day we arrived in France, his logic suggested we ask the largest of the press contingent. He selected a hugely rotund fellow who must have tipped the scales at close to 150 kilograms.

'To get as fat as that in France he must back a lot of winners,' was Bluegum's dubious but not totally illogical deduction. Because I had a rudimentary knowledge of French from my high school days, I was chosen to seek out the selections. '*Nous sommes journalistes Australiens,*' I introduced ourselves to the fat guy.

He gave us a big welcome, but then I stumbled over how to ask for tips. While I was pondering, Mordey blurted out, '*les egg flips, les egg flips*'. His use of rhyming slang only confused the French pressman even more, but I finally hit upon, '*votre selectionnes s'il vous plait*' (your selections, please).

The Fat Frenchman, as Mordey tagged him, was in devastating form, and coming to the last race Bluegum was around $6000 ahead. 'Where are they racing tomorrow?' Bill asked me. 'I saw in the paper that there is a meeting on at a place called Saint Cloud,' I told him, 'but Australia plays England tomorrow so you won't be there.'

I added. 'Listen, Pigeon, if the fat guy's tip wins the last I'll be at Saint Cloud and you'll be at the footy covering the match under my name,' retorted Mordey. 'I've spent my whole life looking for a genius tipster and it looks like I've had to come 10,000 miles to find one, but I have.' Of course the French pressman's final tip ran nowhere, Mordey lost his $6000 winnings and he reverted to Plan A, covering the football for the *Daily Mirror*.

Probably the safest tip is when it is accompanied by the tipster putting plenty of his own cash with it, but even that doesn't always work out. Back in 1988 a dog trainer from Orange named Jack Pringle arrived at Wentworth Park with a greyhound called Worth Doing. The dog was a bush fifth-grader having his first race in the city but Pringle approached Ray Hopkins, then a leading bookie at the dogs, and asked him to put $20,000 on the dog on his behalf.

'This is every dollar I have in the world but this dog is a champion, he is the best I have ever put a lead on,' Pringle told Hoppy, adding: 'He can't be beaten.' That wasn't a bad wrap as Pringle had trained a swag of stars over the previous 20 years, so Hopkins and another bookie pal of his, John Stollery, decided to match Jack's $20,000 with $10,000 each of their own. That meant $40,000 went on this bush dog, but as if to again prove there are no certainties in racing, he got beaten. I've been watching greyhound races since 1963 but to this day have never seen a greater certainty beaten than Worth Doing was that night at Wentworth Park. Everywhere he went another dog seemed to run out and knock him down. After giving the leader about 10 lengths start on the home turn, Worth Doing flew home but went under by a nose.

Pringle, broke and forlorn, sold the dog immediately after the race. Worth Doing then went on to become one of the sport's all-time greats, winning the 1989 National Derby in race record time and being anointed as the NSW Greyhound of the Year in the same season.

2

The Racing Pigeon Doping Scandal

In February 1988, when I added the weekly wine column to my longstanding daily greyhound form duties, my *Daily Mirror* colleagues used to joke to me: 'If you get hit by a bus there'll be a queue a mile long looking for your job.' I don't know about that but I do consider myself extremely fortunate to have spent my entire working life writing about my two great passions — greyhound racing and wine. Another mate once quipped that if I had become News Limited's brothel editor I would have jagged the trifecta! Still, drinking and gambling was a pretty good double to land.

I reckon it beats covering courts, chasing ambulances or reporting politics. I can honestly say that in six years at Consolidated Press on the Packer-owned *Daily Telegraph* and the past 37 years at the Murdoch-run News Limited, I have always looked forward to arriving at work. And I never thought it would be any different.

I always wanted to be a journalist and for Christmas in 1953 my mum Emily presented me — I was then eight years old — with a Swiss-made Hermes Baby portable typewriter. Dear old mum had placed it on lay-by earlier in the year because at £35 that typewriter was a fortune to her in those days. But she knew I was desperate to create my own pretend newspapers — with the slant on racing — and came up with what is still the best Christmas present I have ever received.

Mum and my father Allan, who had spent World War II in the AIF in the jungles of New Guinea, had no racing or wine background. I have to thank my only sibling, brother Barry, for my introduction to those activities. As a kid Barry used to hang out with an old bloke we all knew as Mr Fox, who had a stable of ponies not far from our home in the northern beachside suburb of Harbord.

Mr Fox and my brother would lead the horses at weekends over to Manly Beach, where children paid something like sixpence for a ride. It wasn't long before Barry had his own pony which he rode in local shows, such as at Brookvale and St Ives, and eventually in the Sydney Royal.

Being only a little bloke, he soon gravitated to racing, becoming an apprentice jockey indentured to a battling trainer called Sid O'Rourke. But Sid, who had stables at the now-defunct racecourse at Moorefield, near Brighton-Le-Sands, seemed more interested in my brother's cheap labour (Barry's wage was £1 per week with every second Sunday off) than in seeing him succeed on the track. After Sid had refused him permission to ride for several other Moorefield trainers, including successful ones like Bob Mead and Arthur Croall, Barry pulled the pin.

He then took up motor racing, beginning his career competing in a touring car handicap on the old Mount Druitt circuit in 1957. At that stage Barry didn't own a car, instead borrowing Dad's two-tone blue Ford Anglia tourer. Dad really doted on that car, forever keeping it washed and polished and with the tyres blackened, never even dreaming of pushing it too close to the speed limit of 30 miles per hour.

One Sunday Barry asked Dad to lend him the Ford Anglia to get to Mount Druitt motor races, where he was supposed to be a spectator. Dad was a kind bloke and readily agreed. On Monday morning I was first out of bed and wandered out into the front yard where Dad's car was parked. Not only was the old man's pride and joy covered in grime and muck, but on each front door was the all-too-clear outline of the number 26.

My dill of a brother had entered Dad's Ford in the touring car handicap and had been assigned number 26. The temporary numbers were applied with Bon Ami, a popular household cleanser of the time. When Barry got home late that night he had the presence of mind to clean the numbers off the doors. But he should have washed the car first because there on each door was the unmistakable outline of number 26 on the clean duco, surrounded by the mud and grime of the Mount Druitt dirt surface.

I tore inside and woke my brother, asking incredulously if he had entered Dad's baby in a race. 'Sure did, and it's got no guts whatsoever, it's legless,' was Barry's response. 'Well you'd better get out there and wash it before Dad gets up or you can forget about ever borrowing it again,' I told him. Barry managed to clean off the dirt — and the outlines of the numbers — before Dad woke up and he was never any the wiser.

Barry eventually graduated to driving sports cars at places like Oran Park and Formula One open-wheelers at Bathurst's Mount Panorama, the Gnoo Blas circuit at Orange and Victoria's Phillip Island. He raced against people like Australia's first world Formula One champion, Sir Jack Brabham, and finished up driving for a works team in Formula Three on the European circuit. That's where my interest in wine was, pardon the pun, fuelled.

In the early 1960s Barry returned after two years racing in Europe and put a bottle of red wine on the dining-room table. Dad was horrified. 'You've gone to Europe and come back a plonko' was the old man's reaction. 'Everyone in Europe drinks wine with their meals, Dad,' Barry told him. 'I'm used to it now.'

It wasn't long before I used any punting winnings to buy wine, usually from the old Farmer Brothers store which was out at Waterloo, a few kilometres from News Limited's Surry Hills office. And it was thanks to punting and to my interest in wine that I made my first overseas trip to France in 1972, where I met my future wife. But more about that later. While I am indebted to my brother Barry for my introduction to the world of racing and wine, he was also responsible for one of the most embarrassing situations my family ever endured.

When he was 12 and I was four, he entered his dog, a multi-breed bitser, in the Brookvale Dog Show. Barry was always full of enthusiasm and typically entered his pooch in every class available — from prettiest pet to ugliest, from most obedient pet to fluffiest. Near the end of the day, he was the proud owner of a white ribbon for third place in the ugliest pet class. As the finale to the show the ring announcer declared it was now time for the 'best family group'.

'Come on, Dad, Mum, grab Jeff, we're all in this,' said Barry, rushing towards the centre of the oval with his dog. I can't believe my father fell for this but the Collersons duly trooped out in my brother's footsteps. As we stood in the middle of the park, out came a woman with a male German shepherd, a female shepherd and six little pups. She was soon followed by a bloke with a male and a female corgi along with three corgi pups. More dog families followed. The ring announcer, noticing our lack of any other dog but my brother's pet, approached my father and said: 'I'm sorry, sir, this class is for the best family group of dogs, not people!'

For a bloke who would run a mile to avoid an embarrassing situation, this was about the worst it could get for my father. After giving my brother a gob full he slunk off Brookie Oval. The worst part was that in those days, everybody knew everybody. Most of those in attendance were locals, neighbours and relatives as well as the lady who ran the corner shop, the butcher, the bloke who owned the newsagency and so on. It took the Collersons weeks to live down the embarrassment of the best family group at Brookvale Dog Show.

Despite that, growing up in Harbord in the late 1940s and early '50s was wonderful. Freddy Jones, who captained Manly-Warringah's 1972 and 1973 rugby league competition winning sides, was a classmate at Harbord and a dozen of us used to play footy every afternoon at Jacka Park, on Oliver Road. Freddy and a kid called Pat Byrne, who later captained Manly-Warringah's reserve-grade side, were the best players so weren't allowed to play in the same side. They were made captains of the two Jacka Park kids' teams and would pick sides for the daily after-school games.

Oddly enough in those days, the poor kids in the most modest houses lived near the beach. The slightly better off tended to live a kilometre or so away from the surf, which had a reputation for being the rough area of Harbord. Families of these poor kids' would have had the last laugh when they eventually sold out, as by the mid-1960s land around Harbord's Freshwater Beach was worth a fortune.

The highlight of living in Harbord was the annual Brookvale Show. Brookie Show, held just before Sydney's Royal Easter, was a big deal in the 1950s. It was considered a stepping stone to the Royal and was staged on Brookvale Oval, now Manly-Warringah rugby league team's home ground. To most of us kids the best part of Brookie Show was Jimmy Sharman's boxing tent.

Sharman had a boxing tent at the Royal too, but at Brookvale we locals would get to see people we went to school or work with get up to fight members of the touring boxing troupe. If someone from the crowd was able to last three rounds with one of Sharman's pugs — usually broken-down old former professionals — he would get two quid. In some years my brother Barry hopped into the action, as long as Sharman had a little flyweight among his entourage.

What a different era that was. Imagine members of the public, without any pre-fight medical check-ups and no doctor present during the bouts, battling it out with professional boxers. Wouldn't the lawyers in today's litigious society have a field day!

But all good things must come to an end and in 1956 my father, who was warehouse manager of DHA (Drug Houses of Australia), was asked to live on the premises of his firm's new offices at Tempe. Although I had misgivings about shifting across the harbour — the famous Tempe Tip was all that separated us from noisy Mascot Airport — the change turned out to be terrific.

When I began Year 6 at Tempe Primary School I met a couple of kids who had racing pigeons. That was something unheard of in Harbord. It wasn't long before I had a loft of birds and had joined Cooks River Pigeon Club, whose clubhouse was at the bottom of where we lived in Smith Street. Although I knew nothing about pigeon racing, the older flyers were only too keen to help the new kid in the area. Some gave me birds to breed with, another lent me a pigeon clock and others let me into their training and feeding secrets.

The general rule was an ounce of feed per bird per day for the sprint team and a little more — usually comprising a mix of maple peas, corn, wheat and sorghum — for the long-distance birds.

Among the club members were several Damon Runyonesque characters, none more so than a wild, big-drinking bachelor named Henry Wilson. Henry pulled me aside one year and told me he was a certainty to win the Grand National, which was the Melbourne Cup of pigeon racing. The birds in the National were to be taken by train to Hay, in the far south-west of NSW, where they were to be liberated. To put all the flyers on a level playing field, nobody was allowed to send more than five birds to the Grand National. This was to stop the big lofts, with several hundred birds in training, being able to overwhelm those flyers with small teams.

Henry selected his best five birds, then confided in me he had been able to secure some 'go-fast tonic' from a local trotting trainer. He generously offered to give me some of his winning dope but I decided it was too risky. The birds were duly released in the early hours of Saturday morning, and I got one of my five home late in the afternoon. I walked around to Henry's place a few streets away to see how he'd gone and he was distraught — he hadn't sighted a single feather. On Sunday Henry was up at dawn to wait for his birds but spent another fruitless day.

By Monday the old bloke who was paid to go by train with the birds and to act as the liberator had called in to say five birds had been found dead in the baskets. Sure enough, the five were all Henry's. 'Shit, mate, what did you give them?' I asked him. 'I did what the trotting trainer does with his horses; I put 10 milligrams down each of their throats before I sent them away,' Henry said.

It turned out Henry's go-fast drug was a strychnine-based tonic. But he neglected to adjust the dosage from what the trotting trainer gave his horses! My bet is Henry's five birds were dead by the time they left Central Station. Certainly when they arrived at Hay rigor mortis had set in. There was no drug testing of pigeons, so while the mysterious death of Henry's birds attracted suspicious gossip nothing more was done.

My secondary schooling took place at Enmore Boys' High, a couple of miles from Tempe. Twice a week I would lug a basket of birds, along with my schoolbag, on the Tempe-to-Sydenham and then the Sydenham-to-Enmore buses I took to get to school. What a different world we lived in then. In the three years I did this not one person — bus drivers included — ever complained about sharing their bus with my feathered friends. Can you imagine anyone being so tolerant now?

By taking the pigeons to school with me (usually only about six or eight of them at a time) I was not only giving my birds a training toss but it also enabled me to produce my first racing formguide.

I handed these carbon-copied guides out to teachers and students when I got to school. There, a classmate named Stan Kemp, who later became a bookmaker, would frame a market on which bird would reach Tempe first. In my typed formguide I would give my tips and comments for each bird, with the staff and pupils betting enthusiastically with Stan. Because it was such a short flight the pigeons would invariably arrive home together, so it was a matter of whichever bird was first into the loft being declared the winner.

My mum's task was to stand outside the loft and await the birds' arrival. She knew each bird by name and a blue chequer called Zorro soon established a six-flight winning streak. Zorro, a hen due to a mistaken case of identifying the correct sex by yours truly — pigeons are hard to pick — was usually an odds-on favourite and her wins had most of the kids in clover and Stan on the breadline. At the 11 am recess we would all rush down to the corner shop where I would phone Mum to find out which bird had won. I'd shout the winner's name — usually Zorro — to the assembled throng and the successful punters would order a slap-up lunch accordingly, with the losers going without their sandwiches.

One day a stray bird entered my loft. Essential to the birds' training routine were forced 30-minute, twice-daily-exercise flights around the loft. For several days the newcomer, which I had named Rocket, beat Zorro through the traps when the 30 minutes were up.

Stan saw this as a chance to recoup all his lost money. He asked me to bag Rocket in the formguide but my conscience wouldn't let me do that to my other schoolmates. Instead I gave Rocket a wrap when she was having her first race from school, saying she had been 'trialling brilliantly'. But Zorro's legion of fans ignored my tip, plunging their shillings and two-bobs on their pin-up bird.

To Stan's horror, Zorro, who had been beaten by Rocket in every trial flight leading up to this race, won when it counted. When I phoned Mum to ask her the result she replied: 'Zorro won as usual.' Stan was dumbfounded and had to borrow money from his parents to settle his bets.

I had a bit of success at the pigeon caper but I can tell you that caring for these winged wonders is harder than training greyhounds or probably racehorses. Sometimes a horse or dog trainer believes his animal might stay — that is, be suited by a long-distance race — and tries him accordingly. If the horse or dog fails to get the new journey there's no harm done, the trainer simply reverts to sprint racing again. But you can't do that with pigeons, as I found out to my dismay.

Around 1962 I had a beautiful red chequer cock which I named Time and Tide, after a famous racehorse of that era. Time and Tide won a race from Marulan to Sydney (86 miles as the crow — or pigeon — flies) beating a field of 700 starters. He won the same race the following year, this time leaving 600 birds in his wake. Mel Mercer, the most successful flyer in my years at the Cooks River Pigeon Club, advised me not to be greedy and to put Time and Tide aside for the same race the next year. 'This is obviously the bird's pet distance and his metabolism must be such that he hits his peak around this time of the year,' was Mel's sage advice.

'No way, Mel,' I said. 'Time and Tide wouldn't have blown a candle out after the Marulan race, I'm getting him ready for the Cootamundra Combine.' The Coota Combine was a major race but was 100 miles longer than the Marulan sprint. Full of confidence, I dispatched Time and Tide to the big event and have never seen him since. Seems he could only sprint after all!

My fastest bird was a blue chequer hen called Jessie, but she had one bad habit. She could out-fly most of her race opponents, but when she arrived home at Tempe was reluctant to come into the loft. She was a bit like a slow beginner at the dogs, always finding a way to get beaten. One Saturday she got me into trouble with my father when she landed on the roof of the Drug Houses of Australia boardroom, which was adjacent to our home.

Anxious to get her into the loft to have her race time registered, I hurled a rock at the boardroom. I missed and the stone smashed a window. Fortunately, Dad had a key and was able to retrieve the rock and have the glass replaced before the directors arrived for work the following Monday.

A lot of people bag pigeons, but to me they are the athletes of the bird world. And they are just about the only thing that I won't eat at a restaurant. When I go to Tetsuya's the staff always know to substitute a dish for me when they have squab — baby pigeon — on their degustation menu.

Nobody seems to know how pigeons find their way home, but the method of timing them is well organised. When I was racing, a surveyor would measure the distance from each loft to the Sydney GPO. From that information was gleaned the exact distance from the various race points to the different flyers' lofts. For example, if I lived two miles closer than Bill Bloggs and if the birds averaged 60 miles per hour on race day, my bird had to beat his by at least two minutes. At a week old a metal ring, on which was encoded a serial number, year of birth, and the club's initials, was pushed onto the bird's leg. As the bird grew this ring could not be removed. On the night the birds were dispatched to the race point, a numbered rubber ring was placed over the other leg, which was then listed alongside the metal ring number.

When the first bird arrived home, I would pull off the rubber ring and place it in the pigeon clock, which had been sealed by club officials. A turn of a handle would punch the bird's time on a paper roll inside the clock. On race night each club member would check their clock against the correct time and a gaining or losing clock would have its time adjusted. From all this the placings would be ascertained.

There was even official betting on the pigeon races. These were called pools and were a way of testing a pigeon flyer's judgment. If you were especially confident about a particular bird, you could enter it in the pools section of the race. For various amounts, beginning at around five shillings and going up to £5, you could back a particular bird. It didn't have to win the race, just be first home among all the birds entered in the pool. The pools were on a winner-take-all basis.

Training pigeons was just like training any other racing animal. When birds were really fit they indicated their readiness to fly a great race by the way they were on their toes, feathers gleaming, in the loft. Other more doubtful methods of picking a potential winner were finding a little blood blister running up and down a bird's keel (breastbone) and eye-sign, where part of a bird's pupil spread into the rest of its eye. Some believed in these indicators, others didn't.

While they were not used much in Australia, there have always been non-drug methods of getting a bird to come home quickly. Pigeons mate for life and in places like Belgium (the world home of pigeon racing), England and France, flyers would separate a cock and a hen the day before a race. They would then place the cock's mate with another cock, in full view of the soon very agitated male. A favoured system in Europe was to time it so a hen was sitting on eggs which were about to hatch. The hen would then be removed and sent off to a race. It's a pretty cruel way of accelerating a bird's progress, but apparently it worked, with the anxious hens rushing back home without delay.

3

My First Big Punting Win — on the Draught Races

Sadly, the pigeons had to go when I started work. After completing my Leaving Certificate — in the early 1960s the equivalent of the Higher School Certificate — I managed to land a job as a copy boy at the Sir Frank Packer-run *Daily Telegraph*. Because my hours included Saturdays, which was pigeon race day, I had to sell up and pull down the loft. But it wasn't long before I had a new racing passion: greyhounds.

After a stint as a general copy-cum-messenger boy, I was transferred to work in the sporting department. My pay was £6 a week but I reckon I'd have paid Sir Frank that amount to work in those fabulous surroundings. Most of the racing writers hated typing pre-race comments on the horses; they preferred writing stories. One of them, Ken Harkness, often came to work hungover on a Monday morning following a big night at his local watering hole, the Lawson Golf Club, in the Blue Mountains. Ken would pay me a quid to type out his comment duties for the following Wednesday's races while he had a snooze in the corner. If ever there was a labour of love, this was it. After all, I'd been typing imaginary comment in my own formguides for years.

By late 1963 I had been given a cadetship, and because I got on well with the racing staff I was 'indentured' into the sporting section. The racing writers at that time comprised John Schofield, Jack Lawson (who couldn't type, and wrote his stories, even his race form, by longhand), Neville Prendergast (who later quit to become a successful racehorse trainer), Keith Robbins (whose father Snowy was a famous fight trainer) and Ray Alexander (later to become secretary/manager of the Australian Jockey Club).

The greyhound writer was Mike Gibson, but a few months into my cadetship Gibbo switched to rugby league due to the impending retirement of George Crawford, the doyen of league writers. I don't think I ever saw George without a cigarette stuck on his lower lip, bobbing up and down as he talked. Gibbo's move to league left the greyhound tipster's spot vacant and, as fate would have it, the job was foisted onto me.

All of the above, and yours truly, were forced to comply with a Sir Frank Packer edict that hats were to be worn to the races at all times. *Telegraph* journos were the only ones who had to wear hats to Randwick, Rosehill, Canterbury and Warwick Farm, but to be seen without a chapeau meant instant dismissal. I hated wearing a hat and when I quit Consolidated Press to join Rupert Murdoch's News Limited in 1968 I had a celebratory drink that I would no longer have to don headwear at the track.

The racing writers at the *Tele* were all terrific blokes, but Jack Lawson was the real character among them. He lived in a magnificent two-storey place at Roslyn Gardens, in Elizabeth Bay, and was the guy who recommended to the powers that be that I be promoted from copy boy to cadet journalist. Jack was a classic. He claimed to have taught Nureyev how to dance, Jesse Owens how to run, Bade Didrikson how to play golf, and Yehudi Menuhin how to play the violin. And he had an amazing general knowledge to back up all his outrageous claims.

He would also pick a fight in an empty house. His love of an argument was never better illustrated than one night in the pub when a knockabout from the *Daily Mirror* named Lionel Rankins was drinking with us. When Lionel said that he had always found Chinese women especially sexy, Ranko innocently mentioned that the greatest lover he ever had was Chinese, and that she had 'massive tits'. Jack immediately called him a liar, saying: 'I know you're lying because Chinese women don't have large breasts.' When Ranko retorted: 'Bullshit! I used to suck on them every night so I ought to know how big they were,' Jack came back with: 'Wait a minute, I could be wrong. Was she from the Tsinghai Province?' 'How the hell would I know?' Ranko said. 'As far as I was concerned she was from Bankstown.' Jack then explained that the farther north you get in China, nearer to Mongolia, the bigger the women's breasts become. And Tsinghai apparently is well to the north.

As well as doing the dogs I also covered some of the minor fights at Sydney Stadium. I had always been a keen fight fan, as a kid attending Leichhardt and Sydney stadiums to watch boxing and wrestling. One of the most memorable stoushes I saw at Sydney Stadium involved George Barnes, the British Empire welterweight champion, and his arch rival Darby Brown. The top wrestlers of the time included Al Mills ('The Canadian Lumberjack'), Chief Big Heart, Doctor Jerry Grahame and Gorgeous George.

In those days I could only afford a seat in the bleachers — the seats up in 'the gods' which were a long distance from the ring. Now here I was, a year after leaving school, sitting at ringside in the press seats and being plied with sandwiches and soft drinks by Sydney Stadium manager Harry Miller (no relation to Harry M. Miller). It was a dream come true.

While Keith Robbins was the *Daily Telegraph* boxing editor (he later became turf editor too) he often sent me to substitute for him when a lesser bout was scheduled. I got to cover fights involving the likes of Sid Prior, the brothers Danny and Billy Males and the Americans Ralph Dupas and Ray Perez. I got to know Dupas and Perez and they were terrific blokes. Perez migrated to Australia, and as far as I know still lives in Sydney.

The Stadium was an atmospheric place, with a revolving stage for concerts in the centre of what was essentially an old tin shed. The motor of that revolving stage was once burned out when Bill

Mordey, at the time the *Daily Mirror* boxing writer, and the Stadium manager and promoter Harry Miller decided on an impromptu concert. One Monday fight night, after all the fans had left, Mordey and Miller had a few drinks in the manager's office. Mordey wanted to hop up onto the stage and do a bit of singing, so Miller obliged, even turning on the microphone and the stage mechanism. Later they both went home, rather inconveniently forgetting to switch off the power operating the revolving stage.

The next day, with a concert scheduled for that night, Miller was horrified to find the motor completely burned out. Repairs could not be carried out in time, so the singer involved was told to constantly turn around so all the fans got equal glimpses of his face.

A few years back Terry Smith, later a colleague when I worked for the *Daily Mirror*, wrote a history of Sydney Stadium, *The Old Tin Shed*. In researching his book Terry managed to track down the chauffeur for Lee Gordon, who was Australia's top showbiz promoter of the 1950s and 1960s. And from the chauffeur he heard a classic yarn of when Frank Sinatra was appearing at the Stadium.

Gordon, a larger-than-life character, was a complete desperate but really hit it off with the quirky Sinatra, who even flew to Australia to be best man at one of his weddings. Smithy's Sinatra tale told of how the great crooner insisted on being given oral sex before he began each show. 'It relaxes me,' Sinatra assured Lee Gordon. So Gordon organised for a succession of ladies of the night to be available until one evening the booking failed to show up. Sinatra was becoming agitated until a female friend of Gordon's phoned his office.

'Please, Lee, is there any chance you could organise for me to meet Frank Sinatra after the show? I'll be in your debt forever,' she cooed into the phone. 'How would you like to meet him before the show,' was Gordon's rapid-fire reply. So Frank got his relaxation therapy and went on stage to sing like never before.

It must rank as a miracle that the Stadium was never burned to the ground, with the loss of hundreds of lives. The most expensive seats were called ringside, the middle seats the terrace, with the elevated bleachers no more than long curved planks at the rear. People threw newspapers onto the ground several metres below the bleachers, and with smoking permitted the Stadium must have been the greatest fire trap never to go up in flames.

When I began my cadetship at the *Tele* there were some larrikins among the journos, but the really Runyonesque characters were among those who enjoyed the company of newspaper people. Two terrific characters I encountered early on were the Broadcaster, so called because of his penchant for doing phantom calls of horse races, and Arthur Harris, who wrote a racehorse breeding column under the pen name Tim Whiffler. There were no security passes in those days, and people like the Broadcaster could walk in and out of the *Telegraph* building unchallenged.

Whenever one of Lee Gordon's musical extravaganzas was coming up at Sydney Stadium, the Broadcaster did a bit of casual work for him. One night while I was studying page proofs around 9.30, the Broadcaster phoned asking me to join him at the nearby King's Head Hotel, on the corner of Elizabeth and Park streets.

'I must produce a rock 'n' roll singer as soon as possible,' he explained. 'I have this girl with me and can get a date with her if I can come up with a rock singer. I've explained I work for Lee Gordon, who is about to bring out some big stars. She wants to meet them and she will, but to clinch the deal I got carried away and told her Lee has discovered a rock 'n' roll singer called Dean Florence, from Salt Lake City, Utah. I've told her he's to be the introductory act for this next big show and that he has already arrived in Sydney. She wants to meet you, Dean!' the Broadcaster screamed down the phone.

The last thing I felt like doing was knocking off work for an hour and impersonating a rock 'n' roll singer, but the Broadcaster was too good a mate to refuse. Next minute, there I am in the King's Head, pretending to be Dean Florence, who had already enjoyed a couple of minor hits in the US, and regaling the girl with the benefits of living in Salt Lake City.

The Broadcaster relished using aliases, which he collected through watching the Midday Movie on TV. He would write down any unusual but impressive-sounding name, which often belonged to the hairstylist, the best boy, the key grip or a producer's driver. His favourites were Foxhall Delahunty, Bentley Hodge III, Harcourt Matthews Junior, Randolph Gilbert Junior and Lodge Froschel, names which he used at various times for all sorts of mysterious activities. The Broadcaster and Tim Whiffler would often accompany me to the Harold or Wentworth Park dogs on Saturday nights.

On one occasion the Broadcaster had a bad day at the races and was short of funds for his night at the dish-lickers. Ever resourceful, he parked himself outside a building in Castlereagh Street which housed a Greek restaurant on the first floor and an SP bookmaking business on the second. There was no TAB in those days, so punters who could not get to the track had to bet with illegal SP bookies. The Broadcaster bailed up people about to enter the Greeks' and inquired if they were going for a meal. If they said no and seemed hesitant, he declared the SP joint had been raided, that he was taking all bets on the Greek owners' behalf and that winning wagers would be paid out after the final race of the night. Dozens tumbled for this ruse, giving the Broadcaster money in return for a hastily handwritten receipt. Usually it would state something like, 'John from Kogarah, £10 on Black Top in race four at Harold Park'. Of course all hell would have broken loose when the winner backers turned up later that night to collect bets about which the Greek bookies knew nothing.

Arthur Harris had been discovered by David McNicoll at a party. David, who was avidly interested in racing, had owned a couple of horses and had been spellbound by Harris' encyclopedic knowledge of the breeding side of horse racing. He immediately signed Arthur up to write regular breeding columns for the *Tele* under the nom-de-plume Tim Whiffler — the name of the 1867 Melbourne Cup winner.

Tim, as he became known, was a fascinating character. When discovered by McNicoll he was a lecturer in Sociology at the University of New South Wales. He gradually gave that away to concentrate on racing and became a successful punter. In the early days he also advised The Legal Eagles, the most famous racehorse betting syndicate of the 1960s. The Legal Eagles comprised Bob Charley (later to become chairman of the august Australian Jockey Club), solicitor Morgan Ryan and form analyst Don Scott.

Tim's knowledge of breeding also placed him in a sound position to advise some of the big owners of the day, among them Stan Fox and to a lesser extent his boss, Sir Frank Packer, on which yearlings to purchase. But while Tim was probably the most intensely intellectual character I have ever met, as with many a genius there was a slightly eccentric edge to his character. One Saturday the dogs had been cancelled due to rain, so on the way back to the office from the horse races Tim invited me to his Manly home for a night of draught racing. 'What's that?' I asked.

'Oh, another university lecturer and I race draughts along a glass table and bet on them,' Tim casually replied. 'It works like this. We tilt the table at a slight angle, line up several draughts on their edges behind a ruler, and when all bets are on we take the ruler away. Each of the draughts is painted in racing colours and has a name. I know you did no good on the punt today, Pigeon, so I'll let you into a little secret. I have a certainty at the draught races tonight so you should be there.'

I couldn't believe what I was hearing, but with nothing better to do co-worker Ray Alexander and I arrived for a really quirky night out. Tim pulled me aside and told me: 'Don't have a bet until the hurdle race!' Sure enough, 20 minutes later Tim and his draught-owning rival from uni were taping strands of wool every few inches along the table. These were to be the hurdles.

Tim whispered to me to back a draught called Hiranyakasipu, apparently named after some Indian deity. As the field was being lined up, Tim inquired of his friend about a price for

Hiranyakasipu. 'It's the slowest draught you've got, you can have 10/1,' was the reply.

Tim nudged me so I put £2 on at 10/1, with Tim then plunging 50 quid on this mystery draught. When the race began, some of the other draughts wobbled as they hit the hurdles while others toppled over. But Hiranyakasipu, which Tim had been secretly trialling over the wool, was slow on the flat but must have had the right balance for hurdles. It won easily and I collected £20, the equivalent to a week's pay!

A few days later Tim arrived at the office and asked if I would like to accompany him to David Jones department store to buy some new draughts to increase his 'racing team'. I agreed but was taken aback when Tim asked the shop assistant for a box of each brand DJ's carried. Tim then began rolling the draughts along the glass-topped counter in the Elizabeth Street store, much to the incredulity of the staff. Draughts which were not well balanced and wobbled were hastily returned to their boxes. Within a few minutes there was a crowd around us, and I, red-faced with embarrassment, bolted. I never did find out if Tim obtained a new set of suitable draughts that day, as the night of the hurdle race was my one and only experience of this wacky form of racing.

Tim might have been a tad eccentric but he possessed an amazing knowledge of racehorse breeding genetics and an incredibly quick mathematical brain. One day at Rosehill races I asked him what horse he had backed. The race was a short four and a half furlongs (900 metres) for two-year-olds and there were 24 starters, yet Tim had managed to back 17 of them to show a profit irrespective of which of his bets won. He had wagered various amounts according to each horse's price, something he often did.

But his real strength was his knowledge of thoroughbred genetics. Forty years ago there was a top-class staying horse called High Principle, who ran second in the 1966 Sydney Cup. One Wednesday at Canterbury, Tim almost had an orgasm as the field came out to be paraded before a six-furlong (1200-metre) two-year-old race. 'Pigeon, this horse General Command is a brother to High Principle having his first start, but he is much faster,' Tim shrieked. 'How do you know that?' I asked.

'Because he has one white foot at the back, something High Principle didn't have,' said Tim. 'And going back a hundred years, every champion horse from this family has had one white foot at the back.' However, Tim didn't always temper his knowledge with logic. The race was far too short for General Command, who was bred on stout staying lines, and he ran fifteenth. Tim lost a lot of money on him that day, but his prediction turned out to be totally accurate. When he was switched to long-distance racing, General Command proved vastly superior to High Principle, winning the 1967 AJC Metropolitan at Randwick and the 1968 Sydney Cup.

While Tim Whiffler's draught races and my racing pigeons might have been the most unusual things I've bet on, a running race I contested comes in a close third. In the early 1960s the *Telegraph* sporting staff played a weekly social game of tennis at the famous White City courts, near the Sydney Stadium at Rushcutters Bay. Among the players was the *Telegraph*'s Mike Agostini. Agostini had become its athletics writer after winning the 100-yard gold medal for Trinidad at the 1954 Commonwealth Games in Vancouver and being a finalist in the 100 and 200 metres at the 1956 Melbourne Olympics.

One day after tennis, Agostini declared me the slowest player of our motley crew. 'You're so slow, I reckon I could race you on one leg and win,' he said. When he assured everyone he was serious, the bets went on. Agostini accommodated us all, with the biggest bet on me coming from Keith Robbins, a keen punter. Punchy, as Keith was known, could not believe anybody, even a Commonwealth Games sprint star, could race on one leg and beat a two-legged runner.

We competed over 75 yards and I went straight to the lead. But after about 20 yards Agostini, hopping, left me in his wake, much to the annoyance of my colleagues who had all put their cash on me. 'Agostini is right, you are one legless fucking Pigeon,' shouted

Punchy. 'He must have put his other foot down,' I countered. 'He couldn't have hopped all the way and won.' After being assured that Agostini had indeed run the entire 75 yards on one leg, the likable West Indian-born former athlete told me that power hopping was one of his pet training methods in the lead-up to the Olympic and Commonwealth games. But that didn't make me feel any better.

One of my fellow cadet journalists at the *Tele* in the early 1960s was Doug Parkinson, now a well-known entertainer. Doug, who lived on the northern peninsula, had formed a rock 'n' roll band and was getting a few gigs at Manly pubs. He shocked me one day when he announced he was quitting journalism to become a full-time rock singer. 'Turn it up, Doug, rock 'n' roll might be a bit of fun but you can't earn a living out of it' was my sage advice.

Luckily for him, Doug ignored my counsel, as he went on to have a string of hit records, in recent years starring in several long-running stage shows, including *Buddy* and *The Wizard of Oz*. However, I did have a hand in his first hit record. Always a keen collector of black American rhythm 'n' blues music, I possessed a record called 'Sally Go Round the Roses' by a US girl group called the Jaynetts. It had been a big hit in America but for some reason had received no airplay here. Doug had secured a recording contract so I advised him to record this song, which would come fresh to Australian audiences. He borrowed my treasured 45 rpm import copy and next thing I knew, Doug and his group had the number one record in the country with their version of the song. Doug and I still keep in contact, and whenever he is interviewed he duly gives the *Daily Telegraph*'s wine and dog man due credit for his first hit record.

4

Ambrose Murray — Australia's Damon Runyon

The greyhound is Australia's oldest domestic animal. The botanist Joseph Banks had a greyhound dog and bitch with him on Captain James Cook's *Endeavour* when it sailed from England in August 1768. The ship stopped in the Dutch East Indies for provisions but the local king refused supply until Banks made a gift of the dog to him. And when Governor Phillip and the first immigrants arrived to colonise Australia in 1788 he brought along some greyhounds to help find game for the dining tables of the well-to-do.

The greyhound is the only specific breed of dog mentioned in the Holy Bible (Book of Proverbs, chapter 30, verse 31) while a marble sculpture, believed to date from 350 BC, which was found in Thessaly, depicted the goddess Hecate with a mare and a greyhound. The British Museum also houses a mosaic (circa AD 500 and found in Carthage) which features a greyhound. But despite its regal lineage the greyhound has, in modern times, become known as the poor man's racehorse. Accordingly the sport has always been inhabited, especially in Australia, by unique, colourful characters.

Most legendary of Australia's greyhound characters is Ambrose Murray, who was born on 4 May 1918. Ambrose began training

greyhounds, as a young assistant to his father Ned and older brother Hubert, in 1927. That was the year mechanical lure greyhound racing commenced in this part of the world. Invented by an American named Owen Patrick Smith, the mechanical lure was first used for a regulation race meeting at Emeryville, California, in 1919. But it was another American, 'Judge' Frederick Swindell, who brought the sport to Australia. Swindell staged the first race meeting at what was called Epping track (now Harold Park, in Ross Street, Glebe) on 28 May 1927. New courses soon opened at Lithgow and Cessnock, with a second Sydney metropolitan track launched in November 1927 at Shepherds Bush (now Mascot).

With the new sport of greyhound racing an instant hit, Ambrose's father Ned was quick to capitalise on its popularity.

He laid down a 300 yard straight track on the banks of a creek which ran through the township of Abermain, next to his home town of Weston, near Cessnock. 'Dad couldn't get a licence for his track but that didn't stop him,' recalls Ambrose. 'He raced every Sunday and there was an average of 10 bookmakers in attendance, among them Lennie Burke, later to become the biggest horse racing bookie in the country. Trainers used to pay sixpence to enter their dogs while dad charged the bookies five shillings to operate.

'Occasionally the police would try and close the track down but they had no success. There weren't many cars of any description in those days and to get to Dad's track the police had to drive past the front door of Jock Stephens, who had greyhounds. If Jock saw the local copper approaching he would wave a white handkerchief, and then the nuns in the Catholic Church a bit closer to the track would ring the bells. Whenever they heard the church bells the bookies bolted.

'Dad transformed the straight track to a horseshoe-shaped track in 1936 and we raced there until 1945. The track was never registered but at one stage there were 32 bookmakers operating and big money would change hands.'

The first dog Ambrose and Hubert owned and trained in their own right was called Smokey Joe.

'We bought him for two quid from a fellow called Mark Passfield but received no registration papers. After Smokey Joe started to trial well and was ready to race our father went around to Mark's place to get the papers. Mark confessed he was embarrassed because the dog had no registration papers.

'Dad demanded our two quid back but Mark wouldn't release the money, preferring to make up a set of papers of his own. In those days the papers were rough and ready. They just had a drawing of the dog concerned with all the appropriate markings. There were no ear-brands or anything like that, just the name of the dog, breeding and whelping date. Mark had somehow got hold of some official registration papers which were blank except for the date of birth. He organised a bogus set of papers for us for Smokey Joe and we entered the dog for a race.

'The dog passed the veterinary inspection but just as Hubert was heading towards the kennels the chief steward called him back. "Hey son," he said, "according to your papers this dog is 11 years old!" Hubert replied quick as a flash: "Yes, I know, but we didn't break him in until he was nine." Smokey Joe won a lot of races for us and put plenty of tucker on the Murray family's table. But by the time he had turned five — his real age — he was past his peak and couldn't keep up. Dad told me to take him up the back and shoot him but I had become attached to Smokey Joe and begged to be allowed to give the dog another preparation. Dad relented and I entered Smokey Joe for a Saturday night meeting at Cessnock.

'My mother Merle stuck with Smokey Joe and had £40 to one with each of three bookies. She had him going for 120 quid, which was a fortune in those days. In 1932 Cessnock had an outside lure; that is, the hare used to run around a rail on the outside fence, which was made of tin. The crowd could lean over the fence and almost touch the dogs as they went past. Coming to the home turn the favourite, a dog named Tune In, was five lengths clear of the field, with poor old Smokey Joe five lengths behind the second-last dog. Just as Tune In looked set to win easily, somebody threw a fox terrier over the fence. Tune In forgot all about the dummy hare and took off after the foxie. The next six dogs did the same but Smokey Joe was so far behind he didn't see the terrier. He kept chasing the lure and got up to win.

'Of course there was no filming of races in those days and the stewards, who apparently hadn't noticed the foxie, declared the race valid and all bets to stand. Mum cleaned up, and you know what,' chuckles Ambrose, 'there are still people to this day in Abermain and Weston who claim it was a member of the Murray clan who threw the foxie over the fence!'

A postscript to the story came the following night when the local priest, Father Marshall, came to the Murray home to deliver the rosary. 'He did this every week, going to different homes in the area each Sunday night,' says Ambrose. 'At the end of the rosary us kids used to chirp up, "and God bless Mummy and Daddy". This night our mother put a rider on it, adding "and God bless the bloke that chucked the foxie over the fence".'

Ambrose became hooked on punting when, at the age of 11, he placed fourpence on Nightmarch to win the 1929 Melbourne Cup. Nightmarch won, netting 1s. 6d. for young Ambrose. His father Ned and brother Hubert were also keen bettors and one day at Maitland, in 1932, the trio backed their dog Condor from 6/1 to 6/4.

Condor won but the stewards, made suspicious by the confident betting plunge, decided to take a urine sample for the purpose of drug-testing the dog. 'Condor was the most timid greyhound I have ever seen,' recalls Ambrose. 'If someone came into our yard he would kick the back of his kennel down to get out, he'd be so frightened. Anyhow, this night at Maitland the officials had no luck getting Condor to piddle in the bottle for them. He was simply terrified of strangers. Hubert offered to get the sample for them but the chief steward scoffed at that suggestion. But after a couple of hours, the veterinary surgeon, whose job it was to obtain urine samples, had come up empty. Finally the exasperated chief steward, faced with being stuck at Maitland until the early hours of the morning, agreed to let Hubert get the sample. Hubert ducked around the corner and urinated into the bottle himself, because he knew Dad had given Condor some go-fast dope.

'Problem was, Hubert and I had been guzzling at an old-fashioned alcoholic drink called Wolfe's Schnapps all night,' recalls Ambrose. 'The drug test came back positive to something that was in the Schnapps and our old man was disqualified for 12 months. Yet when someone teased Dad about his son Hubert causing him to get 12 months, he wasn't concerned. "If they had obtained the sample from the dog I'd have got 12 years!" was the old man's answer.

'Ring-ins were rife in those days too because there were no ear-brands and the registration papers were so rudimentary. I knew a fellow called Dick Sealey who had a dog which won nine maiden races under different names. Dick, who was born in Leichhardt but died in Maitland in the 1960s, was a rogue but a real character of the racing game. He was never suspended or disqualified but was eventually warned off every racetrack in Australia.

'In the early 1970s he went to Grafton horse races where he was set to plunge $40,000 on a racehorse called Ricochet. Ricochet, who was trained in Sydney by Jack Denham, won the 1970 Epsom Handicap at Randwick. When Detective Inspector Frank Lynch, who was the racecourse detective assigned to Grafton that year, noticed Sealey in the betting ring he ordered him off the track. Sealey begged to be allowed to stay until after Ricochet's race, promising to be gone as soon as he collected. Frank Lynch had a grudging respect for Dick and relented.

'Ricochet bolted in and I reckon all the detectives there had a nice win on him too. When Frank Lynch escorted Dick off Grafton he asked him why he was so confident Ricochet would win. "I had the rest of the field tied up, Mr Lynch," was Dick's cheeky reply.'

According to Ambrose, Sealey was the man behind greyhound racing's most famous doping scandal of modern times. 'In April 1969, a special four-dog race over 500 yards was organised at Harold Park, featuring Zoom Top, the all-distance champion of that era, up against the three best sprinters, Rokoko, Sammie Sparrow and Gala's Dream. Dick was desperate to nobble Zoom Top to prevent her winning, as she was certain to be the hot favourite, and for him was the most lucrative target.

'He spent two days waiting outside her trainer Hec Watt's property on the western outskirts of Sydney but was unable to get near the champ. That meant a change of plans so he decided he would have to back Zoom Top and instead nobbled Rokoko and Sammie Sparrow. Dick didn't bother with Gala's Dream, who was a 33/1 outsider and considered to have no hope anyway.

'Gala's Dream went straight to the lead and almost pinched the race, but Zoom Top got up in the last few strides to win. Poor old Rokoko and Sammie Sparrow, both doped to the eyeballs, were tailed off. Dick got a bonus too because when he nobbled Sammie Sparrow, he also doped his kennelmate Amerigo Lady, who was an outstanding stayer. She was racing at the same Harold Park meeting and was a hot favourite in her long-distance race. So Dick backed Quiet Rival, who looked the only danger, and naturally enough she won too.

'He won a stack that night, putting $1400 on Zoom Top at 5/2 and a race later having $3500 on Quiet Rival at 4/1. Of course Dick would also have been well looked after by any bookmakers he included in his scam.'

Ambrose was born a year after Les Darcy's death but the great fighter remained his boyhood idol. 'I could recite a poem about Les Darcy before I could say the Lord's Prayer, and I'm a tyke!' exclaims Ambrose. Les Darcy's youngest brother Joe, the baby of farm labourer Ned Darcy's kids, was also a handy fighter and as a boy Ambrose saw him in action. When he became a promoter, Ambrose began training another good young fighter called Jimmy Darcy, who was no relation. 'Jimmy's first pro fight was scheduled for Newcastle Stadium and Hughie Dwyer, who was the big promoter for Stadiums Limited in our area, suggested we bill him as "Les Darcy's nephew".

'I gave him the go-ahead because we knew it would help build up the crowd, and of course the gate money. Billboards appeared around the northern coalfields advertising the professional boxing debut of Les Darcy's nephew and the local paper even carried a story about him. The stadium was packed on the night but just before the fight Joe Darcy came storming into the dressing room, absolutely livid.

'"You'll be getting a solicitor's letter in the morning, Ambrose," said Joe. "You know damn well this kid is no relation to me and Les." Ambrose tried to shift the blame to Hughie Dwyer, which only caused Joe to add: "Then he'll be hearing from our lawyer too."

'Anyway, within 30 seconds of the fight starting Jimmy Darcy had flattened his opponent. As I was leaving the stadium I got a tap on the shoulder. It was Joe Darcy saying, "You know, maybe that kid could be our nephew!" We never did get that solicitor's letter!

'Jimmy then quit my gymnasium on Cessnock Road, Abermain, and a few months later was set to fight a fellow called George Hyde, whom I trained. Not only did I train George, but I was the promoter of the fight. Naturally I appointed myself as the referee. The fight went the distance and Jimmy was convinced he won. When I gave the decision to George, Jimmy shouted at me: "You big bastard. They warned me I'd have to knock Hyde out to even get a draw!" '

Made a life member of the Australian Labor Party in 1991, Ambrose Murray had begun his working life in the Abermain No. 2 coalmine at Kearsley at the age of 14. School was never for him. 'I attended Abermain Catholic School until I was seven, but got expelled, and then went to Weston Public School, from where I was booted out three years later. By the time I was 16 my reputation was such that if any kid from Abermain, Weston or Kurri Kurri misbehaved, they'd be given a good shaking by their parents and told: "If you don't behave yourself and mend your ways you'll grow up like Ambrose Murray!"

'But that didn't worry me or my father. In fact Dad's early advice to me was to get around to the two-up schools, dice rooms and racetracks and learn. His catchcry was: "Never let your schooling interfere with your education".'

Ambrose worked in the mines for 31 years and from 1951 to 1974 co-hosted an open-line sports show on radio 2HD Newcastle. He recalls: 'It was a successful show but I wouldn't have been any good in these politically correct days. Even back then I had a few problems. One day a listener phoned and told me I was a good talker. I caused a hue and cry among some female listeners when I replied that I was bred to talk because my father was an auctioneer and my mother was a woman.

'My days in the mines had ended on 20 May 1962, when I lost two and a half fingers in a mining accident. I got $10,000 compo but had to pay $4000 in medical bills.' Even then, the larrikin Murray was able to find humour in his misfortune. 'Me and four mates were regulars at a local pub and as I walked in I would always hold my hand up to warn the barman to get five schooners ready,' says Ambrose. 'The first time I did this after my accident the cheeky bastard behind the bar gave us a pint, a schooner, a middy and two empty glasses.'

According to Ambrose, not all the characters living in Abermain and Weston were greyhound trainers. 'I remember two bachelor brothers called Jimmy and Hubie and one day Jimmy announced he was getting married. When he told his brother who he was marrying, his brother was horrified. "You can't marry her, Jimmy," Hubie said, "she has been to bed with every bloke in Weston." Jimmy was unfazed, replying: "I know that, Hubie, but Weston is only a small village".'

The Aussie penchant for giving everyone a nickname seems to be going out of fashion. A pity, given some of the terrific monikers Ambrose's coalmining and wharf labouring mates wore. 'Among the wharfies was the Lawyer, who always had his hand in a case, and Hydraulic Jack, who would lift anything,' says Ambrose. 'The miners included Wheelbarrow, who had to be pushed to work, a heavy drinker called Martin Place, who was always full by lunchtime, and the Deckchair. When work started the Deckchair would fold up. And I trained a mediocre boxer who fought under the name Young Banjo. He soon acquired the nickname Kid Candle because one blow and he was out.'

5

Training My First Greyhound Winner

Newspapers used to be a great place to work. The camaraderie generated among an often disparate group of journos sitting around the same large table bashing away at typewriters was fantastic. It has all changed now, though. Computers have journalists sitting at individual work stations, so the old-style banter and repartee have all but disappeared. And even journos are so much busier now than they were in the glory days of newspapers, so the great characters seem to be disappearing.

That applies to the proprietors too. Blokes like Kerry Packer's father Sir Frank, and Ezra Norton, former owner of the infamous scandal tabloid *Truth*, were rough 'n' tumble bosses with a sense of humour. Peter Miller, who as sporting editor was my boss during much of the 1970s on the old *Daily Mirror*, used to tell a great Sir Frank Packer story. It seems when television was introduced here, Sir Frank appointed Alexander MacDonald as the *Daily Telegraph*'s TV critic. There was just one hitch. MacDonald didn't own a TV set, which, when they came out in the 1950s, cost around £800. A black-and-white Admiral television in the 1950s cost around the same as a caravan — I know because my parents eventually opted to buy a TV instead of the holiday vehicle.

Anyhow, after his first week as a TV critic MacDonald filed his expenses. Included was a bold, almost certainly tongue-in-cheek claim for 800 quid for a TV set. Sir Frank was not impressed, and unsurprisingly put his pen through what he deemed was MacDonald's outlandish bid. The following week MacDonald put in a claim of £5 for a camp stretcher. When asked by Sir Frank why he needed a camp stretcher, MacDonald replied: 'To lie on while I watch television outside Eric Anderson's shop window.' In the 1950s so many Sydney citizens were still without a TV set that, unbelievable as it seems today, dozens used to gather outside electrical stores such as Eric Anderson's and H.G. Palmer's in the city to watch this wondrous new device.

Don Hogg, a former *Sun-Herald* wine critic whom I got to know when I began writing wine for the *Daily Mirror* in 1988, also tells a beaut Sir Frank tale. While working for Consolidated Press in 1973, around a year before Sir Frank's death, Hogg got out of the elevator one day to be confronted by the great man himself. 'I'm on my way home to watch the heavyweight fight between Muhammad Ali and Ken Norton,' Sir Frank said. Hoggie realised instantly that even though Sir Frank owned Channel 9, he was not aware he was about to watch a delayed telecast. Not wanting to embarrass the boss in front of the others in the elevator, Hogg pretended he did not know the outcome of the American bout. But he was put in a spot when Sir Frank asked him who he thought would win. Hogg replied: 'I have a sneaking feeling that Ken Norton might cause an upset.' 'Just as well you're not the boxing writer, you've got no idea,' chuckled Sir Frank, before adding: 'Would you like to make a small wager on the result?' By now Hogg had painted himself into a corner so insisted on a modest bet of $20.

A couple of days later Hogg bumped into Sir Frank and Kerry in the corridor. 'You were right, Hogg, Norton did win,' said Sir Frank, turning to Kerry and saying, 'Give Hogg $20.' Kerry looked slightly bemused but handed over the money. A year later Hogg attended Sir Frank's funeral. He swears that as the hearse pulled away, Kerry tapped him on the shoulder and said, 'Give me that

$20 you owe me.' Obviously Kerry realised Hogg had got set after the bout, but to his credit he didn't shelf the reporter to his old man.

Then there was the classic tale of Sir Frank sacking a kid who didn't even work for him. A young fellow from the rival John Fairfax newspaper group ran an errand to the *Telegraph*'s offices on the corner of Park and Castlereagh streets. He decided to ride up and down in the lift, much to the chagrin of Sir Frank, who was trying to reach the ground floor. When Sir Frank finally stopped the lift and caught up with the teenager, he asked him how much he earned per week. The sharp young bloke replied, 'Six pounds' so Sir Frank gave him 12 quid adding: 'There's this week's and next week's pay. You're fired.' The kid just pocketed his £12 and headed back to the *Sun* and *Herald* offices over on Broadway. How smart is that!

I enjoyed my time working for Sir Frank and David McNicoll on the *Daily Telegraph* but relished even more the move I made to Rupert Murdoch's *Daily Mirror* in August 1968. I was still a cadet journalist when Pat Farrell, then racing editor of the *Mirror*, asked me to switch camps. 'The *Mirror* wants to go big on greyhound racing and I want you to be our dog man,' was Farrell's offer. Pat, nicknamed Bumper after the sobriquet enjoyed by that legendary tough policeman Frank 'Bumper' Farrell, was the epitome of the old-world racing writer.

The story goes that he would drink the best part of a bottle of Jack Daniel's before work each day, but if he did, it never showed in his copy. His daily sports column, 'Sitting Pat', was the best read in Sydney and while he was a tough boss he was fiercely loyal to his staff.

He often defended them by unorthodox means. In my early days on the *Mirror* I had a run-in with Norm Smith, then manager of one of Sydney's two greyhound clubs, the NSW Greyhound Breeders, Owners and Trainers Association. Rex Jackson, later to find infamy and do time in jail after being found guilty of corruption while the NSW Minister for Corrective Services, was the GBOTA patron. Farrell heard that Jackson was trying to make an appointment with Rupert Murdoch to have me sacked. A week later Pat phoned me at home to say everything was sweet.

It wasn't until a decade later, when I was introduced to Sydney's top gambling czar, Joe Taylor, that I discovered how things had been smoothed out. Keith 'Punchy' Robbins, my old *Tele* boss, introduced me to Taylor at his Palace Club, an illegal casino in Macleay Street, Kings Cross. Later Keith came over to me and said: 'Joe knows you.' When I told Punchy that I had never met Joe Taylor, he said: 'He didn't say he'd met you, he said he knew you because he once did you a favour. Apparently he sorted out a problem you had with Norm Smith and Rex Jackson.' It transpired that Pat Farrell, like Keith a great friend of Taylor's, had got the king of the illegal casinos to put pressure on Jackson and/or Smith to leave me alone.

'Old-style policing' was also in vogue in the 1960s and 1970s. During one period a character was going around doping dogs which were hot favourites for big races. He would then get a leading bookmaker or two to offer inflated odds about the nobbled hounds. I began campaigning in the *Daily Mirror*, lambasting the greyhound racing authorities. My articles pointed out that the nobbler's identity was common knowledge but nothing was being done, so the public was being robbed and the sport's credibility ruined. It wasn't long before I was threatened by the culprit.

A pal of mine, a Licensing Squad police sergeant named John, trained a couple of greyhounds as a hobby and heard about my run-in with the nobbler. Not being sure how serious the threat was, I insisted he do nothing official, hoping things would just blow over.

A day later I got a phone call from Detective Sergeant Nelson Chad, at one time chief of the CIB Fraud Squad. 'I believe you have a problem,' Nelson said over the phone. I was astounded, quickly telling him I had asked John not to inflame the situation. 'Don't worry. My call is unofficial,' Nelson replied. 'Listen, son, there are good guys and there are bad guys,' he added. 'John tells me you're a good guy, so you shouldn't have to put up with shit like this. Just tell me where this nobbler drinks and I don't think you'll hear from him again.'

Reluctantly I told Nelson Chad where the dog-doper was reported to hang out. I don't know exactly what transpired, but the next time I saw the nobbler at the track he glanced at me and headed the other way. In these days of rampant crime with police powers largely restricted, many would say that old-style policing was better for everybody.

Apart from those unsavoury incidents, my time on the *Daily Mirror* was so much fun I was probably entitled to pay Rupert Murdoch to let me work there. It was made so enjoyable by the characters in the office at Holt Street, Surry Hills, as well as the larrikins I got to know at the racetrack. Chief racing writer was Ossie Imber, who was remarkably naive for a racecourse habitué. I recall Ossie taking his wife, in 1972, to see the Marlon Brando movie *Last Tango in Paris*. This was the most notorious movie of its time, thanks to the anal sex/butter scene. Poor old Ossie had thought he was taking his wife to a musical!

Our soccer writer was a Englishman called Tony Horstead, who wrote under the pen-name Hotspur. Hottie, as he was known, loved a drink, and would invariably duck out to a nearby early-opening pub for a heart-starter soon after he began his shift at 6.30 am. 'I'm just going down to the library to check some facts,' was Hotspur's usual explanation to the boss as he sauntered out. Nobody really believed the library story, especially one wet morning when Hottie took his umbrella with him for his supposed trip from the fourth to the third floor!

Another character on the *Mirror* staff was Tony Megahey, now the Sideline Eye on 2GB's Continuous Call rugby league team. Megahey, nicknamed Magoo because of his poor eyesight, had a really quick wit. On my first overnight tryst with a girl at a motel, I told my mother I wouldn't be home to sleep as I was going to a party in the city. I told her I would spend the night at Magoo's house, which was closer to town. In those days kids wouldn't dream of telling their parents they were out fornicating.

'Thanks for letting me know, darling,' said my mum. 'Otherwise I would worry.'

Well you wouldn't want to know but I forgot to tell Magoo of my plans for an amorous evening. Next morning, long before I got home, he phoned my house. Mum answered the phone and when she heard the voice on the line said: 'Jeff told me he was staying at your place last night, Tony!' Quick as a flash, Magoo realised I had told my mother a porky and without missing a beat replied: 'Yes he did, Mrs Collerson, that's why I'm ringing you. Listen, he's still asleep. How does he like his eggs done?'

Not long after joining the *Mirror* I was introduced to the world of ghost writers. These are the journos who actually pen the columns for the celebrities and sportsmen whose photographs and by-lines appear above various newspaper columns. At the *Mirror* in the late 1960s and during the '70s and '80s we published columns by people like rugby league legend Johnny 'Chook' Raper, English and Arsenal soccer star Charlie George, champion boxer Rocky Gattellari and Bernie Purcell, who played league for Wests, Souths and Australia from 1948 to 1960.

Bill Mordey or Peter Frilingos looked after Chook Raper's column so well that the Test star, who played for Newtown and St George from 1957 to 1969, seldom knew what he was meant to have written until he bought the paper! Reason was that while Chook was supposed to phone in to supply some newsworthy ideas he could rarely be found at edition time. So Chippy Frilingos or Bluegum Mordey would write his column off the top of their heads. To his credit, Chook never whinged or complained about what they wrote.

Tommy Anderson, who took over from veteran Tony Horstead as our soccer writer, was Charlie George's ghost. But the George column didn't last long. Charlie, who had come to Australia in 1977 to play a season for St George, was a mad greyhound man. On his first day at the *Mirror* office in Holt Street, Ando made the mistake of introducing this soccer ace to me. After that, every time Charlie lobbed at News Limited he'd head straight for my desk to sit and talk about the dogs. Ando naturally took exception to waiting around while Charlie talked greyhounds with me before doing his soccer column.

But the crunch came when Charlie failed to turn up at a gala dinner in the city for which he was the guest of honour. On the way to the function he called in to Wentworth Park dog track to have a bet in the first race. He had intended leaving after that but when I tipped him the winner he decided to stay for one more race. I jagged the second winner too, and by the time race three came around Charlie had well and truly missed the dinner. His column, for which he was being well paid, was punted forthwith.

My sole stint as a ghost writer was doing Rocky Gattellari's boxing column. I got on well with Rocky who became, and still is, a good friend. Rocky, an Australian champion fighter, at least had his own thoughts on what should go into his column. But he had to be curbed occasionally. He would sometimes tell me: 'Write this: that referee who handled Monday night's big fight is an absolute cheat.' I would then have to explain to the Rock that we couldn't actually publish that, but Rocky's column was always interesting and often controversial.

Bernie Purcell, who coached Souths for a while after retiring from playing football, also had real news sense. After retiring from coaching, Sudso as he was called (after the Persil-brand soap powder which had been popular in the 1950s) began working for South Sydney Council. On the day before his column was due he never failed to arrive at the *Mirror* office. He would sit alongside Bill Mordey or Peter Frilingos and offer interesting thoughts on rugby league, with the two journos putting Bernie's perceptions into good English for the widely read Purcell column.

In the early 1980s Bernie gave Les Boyd, then playing for Manly, a real bake. Les took exception to Bernie's criticism of his game and successfully sued the *Daily Mirror*. At the time Brian Hogben, a News Limited executive, informed me how tricky defamation cases could be. 'We've lost some we should have won and vice versa,' Brian said. 'When you go before a jury anything can happen. If a bookmaker is suing a newspaper it can almost come down to who the jurors dislike the most, bookies or newspapers.'

Les Boyd harboured a long-standing dislike of Chippy Frilingos. Years later, I bumped into Les at a wine function. He was back living in his old home town of Cootamundra and working for a liquor company. I had got to know Les through him being a regular at the dogs and getting tips from me. At the wine function, Les asked me: 'How's that arsehole Frilingos going?' I of course jumped to Chippy's defence, saying: 'Les, if you got to know him you'd think the world of him. There isn't a better bloke in the world than Peter Frilingos.' To which Les replied: 'Yeah, I suppose I should let bygones be bygones. Listen, when you see Frilingos, tell him that next time he's down Cootamundra way to give me a call. I'd love to take him shooting!' When I passed on this gem to Chippy he replied: 'Yeah, I bet he would. Only I'd be the target.' I think Chippy was right too.

Peter 'Chippy' Frilingos and Bill 'Bluegum' Mordey died only a week or so apart during 2004. Bluegum had long been a heavy smoker, solid bourbon drinker, and minuscule eater, so his passing was not totally unexpected. But Chippy's fatal heart attack, suffered at his desk, was a complete shock to everyone. Their deaths marked the end of an era in sports journalism.

Anyway, Bernie Purcell became a good mate of mine and did me a huge favour in the mid-1980s when I was set to take my wife Catherine and sons Nicolas and Dion back to France to visit the in-laws and then on to Canada and the USA. Bernie asked me who we were flying with and when I told him, he said: 'Gee I wish I'd known. A mate of mine is the Asia/Pacific boss of that airline and I might have been able to do something for you.' We were leaving five days later but Bernie insisted on me giving him our flight details saying: 'I can't promise anything but I'll see what I can do.' I thought no more of it but when we lobbed at Mascot discovered that the whole family had been upgraded to business class for our round-the-world trip.

I couldn't believe it. Here was council worker Bernie, who

would often turn up at News Limited in his navy blue singlet, shorts and work boots, having enough pull with the boss of an international airline to get a family of four upgraded. When we got back I asked Bernie to explain his connection. He said: 'The airline boss's brother used to have a fruit barrow in Taylor Square. At one stage he was selling stolen watches from there and got arrested. His brother phoned and asked me if I could do anything on his behalf, saying it would kill their parents if he went to jail.' It transpired that an old team-mate of Bernie's at Souths was an inspector in the police force and was able to get the charges dropped. As a result, the airline chief told Bernie he only ever had to ask and he would return the favour many times over. 'I never travel overseas, I don't even go to Manly, so I use his favours for mates like you,' the generous Purcell told me.

Bernie was a great raconteur too. He once related how, at his initial first-grade game for Western Suburbs in 1948, he had a blazing fist fight with Frank 'Bumper' Farrell, who was playing for Newtown. They were each sent from the field by the referee. Later they bumped into each other at the Clock Hotel, in Crown Street, Surry Hills. Bumper, who was a tough old policeman and a real football hardhead, pulled Bernie aside and told him there were no hard feelings. According to Bernie, because they were due to front the judiciary panel a couple of days later, Bumper advised him it would be advantageous for him if he knew what to say.

'Bumper gave me my riding instructions for the judiciary,' Bernie told me. 'He pointed out that he had been sent off plenty of times and had often appeared before the judiciary panel. He claimed he knew how to handle things but because I was only a kid it would be best if I let him guide me on how to approach the matter.' Bernie followed Bumper Farrell's instructions on his judiciary appearance to the letter. The result? Bumper got off scot free and Bernie was suspended for three matches!

Through attending race meetings in the course of my work at the *Mirror*, I became friendly with Tommy 'T.A.D.' Kennedy, a leading horse trainer of his day who later became chairman of the

Sydney Turf Club. T.A.D. (nicknamed 'Try Another Day') gave me my first greyhound, a fawn bitch named Nimble Spinner.

She answered to the pet-name of Dimples, and while a mediocre racer was beautifully bred. She used to roam the fenced-off backyard at the family home at Tempe, where a neighbour's cat often taunted her by promenading along the top of the wooden paling fence. Dimples would leap at the cat but the agile feline always managed to dart away at the last minute. Except early one morning.

It couldn't have happened at a worse time, as I had been to the Journalists' Club, in Chalmers Street, until 4 am. I had no sooner tumbled into Blanket Bay, nursing a massive hangover, than my mum was rousing me. 'Jeff, get up quick. Dimples has caught that cat and there are bits of it all over the yard.' Shovelling up fragments of bloodied cat before the neighbour came to inquire about his missing tabby didn't do a lot for my already seedy stomach.

Like nearly all greyhounds, though, Dimples loved people. A mate used to bring his two-year-old son to our house and the little fellow would ride around on Dimples' back. When Dimples came in season I mated her twice, first with a dog called Best Sun and then with Takiri. To Best Sun she threw a TAB winner called Ivory Smoke, but the Takiri litter was better. I'll never forget when Nimble Spinner was due to whelp. Someone had advised me to put sheets of newspaper in her kennel and every morning she would have them torn into perfectly shaped, narrow strips. And every morning I would chastise her and replace the torn paper with a new pile of broadsheets. That was until somebody at the track informed me that pregnant bitches always tore up paper in order to have something in which to wrap up the afterbirth when the pups arrived.

One morning when Dimples failed to appear in her pen, I investigated and found her suckling six gorgeous little pups. I sold a fawn bitch, later named Roquefort, to Tony Megahey, who had become the greyhound man for the *Mirror*'s rival afternoon paper the *Sun*. A professional trainer named Johnny Munro trained Roquefort for him until I borrowed her, when I headed off for a busman's holiday to the Queensland Cup carnival, held at a track called Beenleigh.

Johnny was an especially gifted greyhound chiropractor, and in more recent years has helped hundreds of sporting stars recover from serious injuries. He has long looked after the physical well-being of the Newcastle Knights rugby league team, and his home in the NSW northern coalfields is adorned with dozens of glowing tributes to his prowess. Andrew 'Joey' Johns, regarded by many as the world's greatest rugby league player, is one of Johnny's admirers.

Andrew Johns first got to know Johnny Munro when the Newcastle Knights coach recommended he get the greyhound trainer to work on some of his injuries. Johns arrived at Munro's kennels, near Maitland, and was told to jump into the hydrobath. 'But there's a greyhound in there,' came Joey's startled reply. 'Don't worry, he doesn't bite, just strip off and get in with him,' insisted Munro.

I love the story of how Johnny, as a teenage kid, got his kick along. He was living not far from Randwick racecourse and a few weeks before the 1940 Melbourne Cup saw a trainer giving a racehorse a hosedown after a workout. 'What's the name of that horse, mister?' asked the inquisitive Johnny. 'Old Rowley,' came the reply, 'and what's more he'll win the Melbourne Cup.' A few days later Johnny was introduced to jockey Andy Knox. He asked Knox if he had a ride in the race that stops the nation. Knox replied: 'Yes, I'm on a horse called Old Rowley and he'll win it too.'

Johnny now had two hot tips for the rank outsider but had no money to back the horse. So he organised a sweep among his family's neighbours, telling every participant they had drawn Old Rowley in the ballot. Sweep sales garnered Johnny a healthy bank which he placed on Old Rowley with an SP bookie at 100/1. When the horse won, John paid out to each of the sweep winners a mere fraction of what he collected from the bookie. How's that for street smarts from a kid?

But I digress. Magoo and Johnny agreed to let me take Roquefort with me to Queensland and she won her Cup heat by 10 lengths. The day before her semi-final I noticed she was bleeding slightly and was obviously coming in season. Old-time trainers always reckoned a bitch on the verge of coming in season would run the race of her life, providing you could sneak her past the veterinary surgeon on race day.

So before kennelling Roquefort I spent 20 minutes painting her vagina with vinegar — according to the old-timers the only sure method of masking her condition. We got past the vet and again Roquefort won by 10 lengths, rocketing to favouritism for the final. But by final day she was in a full-blown seasonal condition and was obviously not the same super-fit greyhound which had won her heat and semi. The vinegar treatment got us past the vet again, but Roquefort, the favourite, ran below her best and was unplaced to a dog called Jim Snell, trained by a current top Queensland trainer named Jack Irwin.

In 2005 I had a good chuckle over another female greyhound, this time one that would not come in season. At the NSW Greyhound of the Year awards, held at Sydney's Star City Ball-room, I inquired from Ray Smith, owner of the award winner

Irinka Barbie, whether his prize bitch had come in season so she could be mated. Her pups were set to be worth a fortune, so it's little wonder Smith, from Forbes, in western NSW, was keeping a close watch on his champion. He replied to my query: 'No, mate, she hasn't come in season yet but I'll tell you what, she has the most gazed upon fanny in Australia. Every morning I jump out of bed, rush down to the kennels, lift up Irinka Barbie's tail and stare at her fanny!'

While I sold Roquefort, I kept one of Nimble Spinner's Takiri pups, a black bitch which I called Soul Baby. I decided to train her myself and she won a few TAB races at the provincials. Her first win, at Cessnock, was easily the most memorable. I had not previously trained a winner I had bred and raised myself, so the buzz when Soul Baby — kennel name Aretha after the soul singer — roared into the catching pen ahead of the field was indescribable. She raced up to me wagging her tail as if to say: 'Didn't I do good!'

In a later Cessnock win she provided my family and a few mates with plenty of laughs. Gary Manning, who worked on the *Daily Mirror*-owned racing paper the *Sportsman* when I arrived at News Limited in 1968, was a bold punter. One Monday night he joined his brother Paul, me, my mother and Soul Baby on a trip to Cessnock. At the time Gary was a chain-smoker but when I caught the whiff of smoke emanating from the back of my old Chrysler Valiant station wagon I ordered him to stop immediately.

Johnny Munro, my training mentor, had warned me under no circumstances to allow anyone to smoke when there was a greyhound in the car. Gary was a bit of a whinger so the thought of spending two hours without a fag really upset him. But worse was to come. Gary was keenly anticipating a visit to his favourite Chinese restaurant, which was at Cessnock. But we got behind a couple of semi-trailers on the trip north and as I wanted to walk Soul Baby around the track before the race we ran out of time for the restaurant. That really cheesed Gary off, and things didn't get any better when he began losing heavily in the early races.

While I was collecting the commission of bets to place on Soul Baby on behalf of his brother Paul and my mum, Gary threw in $30. 'Soul Baby is a million to one but she's spoiled my night completely so she might as well take my last $30,' he moaned. Soul Baby led all the way at the juicy odds of 33/1, giving Gary a $1000 result. Better than that, he then proceeded to bet up and finished up turning the original $30 into close to $10,000. He bought Soul Baby an ice-cream when we stopped for coffee on the way home.

In over 40 years covering the greyhounds I've never met anyone more astute on a racecourse than Gary Manning. He was a genius at working out what was going on in the betting ring and, as sometimes happened, which dogs were actually being trained by somebody more skilful than the name appearing in the racebook. But away from the track Gary sometimes came back to the field. He soon became the proud owner of a Mercedes-Benz 450SL, the top-of-the-range Merc of the time. There was just one problem. Gary didn't know how to put petrol in it.

He would go out of his way to find a garage where pump service was provided, but gradually the self-serve phenomenon spread and he was stymied. Heading for Bulli dogs one night, he was almost out of gas so stopped at the only available station, a self-serve. Gary carefully watched the actions of another customer and filled the Merc without a problem. Halfway down Bulli Pass the car began spluttering and backfiring. Gary had filled the car with diesel, not petrol, and it cost him a small fortune to have the motor repaired.

Like all of us, Gary has his faults, but if you were in the trenches he is the sort of fellow you'd want by your side. He was generous to a fault, and a former trainer told me recently Gary once gave him $5000 after he tipped him his dog when it won a small race at Richmond. On another occasion one of Sydney's leading television personalities spent six months mowing Gary's lawns to repay a gambling debt Gary had settled on his behalf.

Gary had the convoluted nickname of Chevvy. It came about because his middle name was Milton, and the flashest Kings Cross hotel in the early 1960s was the Chevron Hilton. Rhyming slang turned Milton into Hilton, and the hotel prefix Chevron was shortened to Chevvy. When he was on top, money meant nothing to Gary. I recall him paying his brothers Graham and Paul $25 apiece to let him watch his favourite show whenever there was a family dispute over control of the TV. The old black-and-white American crime series *Highway Patrol*, starring Broderick Crawford, was Gary's pet show on the tube and attracted a $50 bounty.

Gary and I often got a ride to the provincial dog meetings at places like Dapto and Wollongong with Jack and Dot Hansell, a lovely old couple who always had a couple of greyhounds in the backyard of their house in Evaline Street, Campsie. Dot would always wrap two bundles of $50 notes in ladies' handkerchiefs, each sealed with a safety pin, which she took to these meetings. The bundles, usually amounting to $500 apiece, weren't for her and Jack as they were small bettors. They represented emergency punting banks for Gary and myself in case we ran out of cash.

Once, before we left for Dapto, Gary and I told Dot not to bring any extra money as it was a poor meeting and we didn't want to be tempted into betting. Jack had the car's motor running, so Dot ran into the yard and hid the money. The next day she couldn't remember the hiding place, which turned out to be at the bottom of one of the greyhounds' feed bins. She discovered her long-lost $1000 about a year later.

There was probably no more colourful character on the *Daily Mirror* when I arrived than Bill Mordey, then the paper's chief rugby league writer. Bill, like Gary, was a fearless punter and also, like Gary, enormously generous. His world revolved around sport and gambling, and he readily admitted he hadn't seen a movie in something like 30 years.

So when I was with Bill and Ernie Christensen, in a London casino during a football tour, Mordey did not recognise the fellow on the other side of the roulette table. He did notice, however, the fellow's statuesque blonde companion. The blonde, with a plunging neckline displaying a pair of bristol cities that would make Dolly Parton look like Twiggy, began eyeing Bill and flirting with him quite outrageously. Mordey pulled Christensen aside and said: 'Listen, when that grubby-looking bloke with the magic wand [blonde] goes to the toilet, I'm going to whisk her out of here. I probably won't be back for a couple of days so get the Pigeon to cover for me at the football.'

An incredulous Christensen retorted: 'Do you know who that so-called grubby-looking bloke is, you poor imbecile?' Mordey answered in the negative, so Christensen pointed out it was Omar Sharif, the male movie heart-throb of the time who a few years earlier, in 1962, had been one of the stars in *Lawrence of Arabia*. 'I don't think she'll be dumping Omar for the football writer from the Sydney *Daily Mirror*, so get back to concentrating on the roulette,' was Christensen's to-the-point advice.

Mordey of course later found fame as a boxing promoter, launching the professional careers of greats like Jeff Fenech and Kostya Tszyu. He even co-promoted some Australian fights, shown around the country on hotel and club television sets, via Sky Channel, with the notorious American promoter Don King.

After one big fight King phoned Mordey to check up on whether all the hotel and club owners had coughed up their fee for being given the rights to televise the bout. Mordey told King all the money had arrived but that the owner of a tiny hotel somewhere in far north Queensland had refused to pay. 'It's only $200 so it's not worth worrying about,' was the easy-going Mordey's stance. King was horrified. He replied: 'Bill, if word gets around they can get away with not paying, you'll have a dozen refusing to settle next time. This is a matter of principle so I'll send a couple of my boys out to visit this fellow. Don't worry, after they visit him he'll pay up.' Horrified at the prospect of a couple of heavies from New York monstering some pub owner in far-off Queensland, Mordey asked King to give him another week to obtain the money. Mordey then paid the $200 himself in order to avoid a dangerous confrontation.

6

Greyhound Betting Rorts

Pat Farrell was true to his word when I moved from the Packer-owned Consolidated Press to Rupert Murdoch's afternoon tabloid the *Daily Mirror* in 1968. He expanded the greyhound racing coverage and with it I became more involved in the sport, getting to know a whole new world of wonderful characters — comprising owners, trainers, bookmakers and punters. Two of the most colourful trainers were Cliff Abraham and Bobby Carter.

Unusually for a dog trainer, Abraham was always immaculately dressed in a well-tailored suit and tie. He effused charm and soon had the run of the *Greyhound Recorder* newspaper office. The *Recorder*, the bible of greyhound racing in those pre-computer days, provided the formguide/racebooks for all non-metropolitan race meetings. The office was stacked with alphabetically listed form cards for every greyhound. When the fields for a country race meeting were drawn up, the *Recorder*'s clerks would assemble the form cards for each race and the appropriate racebooks were printed.

One year Cliff had a very fast unraced maiden he was setting for a race at the Grafton carnival in July, a bush meeting renowned for its big betting activities. The only problem was that book-makers would be wary about betting extravagant odds about an unraced maiden in the name of Cliff Abraham, who had the reputation of being an astute trainer. Abraham was renowned for the ability of his dogs to pull off spectacular betting plunges, so rather than arrive at Grafton with a mysterious unraced pooch he helped himself to one of the *Greyhound Recorder* office's blank form cards. He then filled out the card with three bogus unplaced runs for his 'hot maiden'.

In order not to arouse suspicion among Grafton locals, clever Cliff listed the dog's flops as being at cricket-score odds at tracks as far away from the northern rivers course as possible. Because of his dog's poor record, as it appeared in the *Greyhound Recorder* racebook for Grafton, Cliff got double-figure odds about the hound. It was backed off the map into odds-on favouritism and won easily. *Greyhound Recorder* editor Jack Woodward soon got wind of the ruse and Cliffy's entry to the newspaper's office was barred.

In the late 1960s Bobby Carter had a big team in work and had a bright idea when he saw me trialling a greyhound called Blue Plum, which I was training as a hobby. 'Gee she's got some early pace, you should nominate her for a 300-yard race at Tamworth, she'd be a certainty,' was Bobby's advice. 'I'm not going all the way to Tamworth with one dog to race for $100 prizemoney,' I replied. 'No, come up with me and the boys, we'll have a few dollars on her and make a day out of it,' said Bobby.

So I entered Blue Plum and took her across to Bobby's kennels at Hoxton Park, near Liverpool in Sydney, to get a lift with him in his panel van. It was crammed with greyhounds, and as we headed north I expressed my doubts as to Blue Plum's ability to win. 'Well, she'll beat that brindle dog in the back of the van,' said Bobby. 'And she's sure to finish in front of the black bitch as well as that big white and fawn dog.' To my astonishment, most of the dogs in the back of the car, all trained by Bobby or his associates, were in the same race as my greyhound. I soon realised that Blue Plum was the pea as Bobby had managed to get her into a race with three of his team, which on this day anyway, were deemed to have no chance. We came unstuck, though, with a local dog tipping Blue Plum out in a tight finish.

Bobby also delights in a story that dates back to the 1950s,

when as a kid he attended Goulburn dogs. Bob's father Harry was involved in the training of a couple of litter sisters owned by big betting Phil Metham, whose Metham Motors was one of Sydney's largest car dealerships. The greyhounds, Silent Worker and Power Dive, were identical, and just to make things really interesting, their ear-brands differed by just one letter.

But there was a yawning gap in their relative speeds. Silent Worker was an outstanding, top-grade city sprinter while Power Dive was, in Bobby's words, 'legless'. At Goulburn, Power Dive was first to compete, in a maiden race, and because of her dismal form was scorned even by her connections and sent out as a 33/1 chance. Only Bob's dad Harry, betting with his head and not his heart, stuck fast and had £30 on her at the mammoth odds. Fortuitously for Harry, the kennel's handler mistakenly brought Silent Worker out of the kennels for the maiden race. Some slovenly cross-checking of her ear-brand with her identification papers resulted in the top-notcher competing under the name of Power Dive. Naturally, 'Power Dive' blitzed her maiden-class rivals, winning by 25 lengths — and netting a cool £1000 for Harry.

However, this left Metham and his pals with a bit of a problem, as they had been keen to plunge on Silent Worker in her correct race. Aware the champion greyhound had already contested a 500-yard race earlier in the afternoon, they were now too frightened to bet. To scratch Silent Worker would be to admit the error by the kennel's handler, which could have resulted in a fine or disqualification. So Silent Worker took her place in the top-grade sprint and, drifting in the betting after being unbacked by her connections, proved just how good she was by still trouncing her rivals.

Greyhounds can show remarkable stamina as I've known of other dogs who, like Silent Worker at Goulburn, have made light work of having two gallops in one day. At Cessnock in the early 1970s a friend had a greyhound making her debut in a 617-metre middle-distance race. She had trialled brilliantly but my mate was filthy that a track tout — a professional punter who clocked track gallops — had almost surely recognised his dog.

He therefore decided to stop his greyhound from winning. He first gave her an hour's galloping through the sandhills near his home before heading for Cessnock. Then, on the way to the starting boxes, the trainer jammed her muzzle into her face and smeared petroleum jelly across her eyes. Despite having restricted breathing and sight — and greyhounds hunt and chase by sight, not smell — my mate's greyhound stormed down the outside to win.

Unless greyhounds are attempting to qualify for a special race by contesting official non-betting heats, they are trialled anonymously. However, a small band of touts have for years made a living by attending these trials — currently at Wentworth Park they are held Tuesday mornings and Thursday nights — and having the skill to identify those participating. The markings of all trial dogs are logged into a book, along with size, any unusual traits, and of course, if possible, the identity of the handler.

Some touts even had an assistant with a walkie-talkie placed near the exit gate. If a dog and its handler were impossible to pinpoint, the assistant's role was to jot down the numberplate and make of the car in which they left the track. After that, an acquaintance at the Motor Registry Department would match the numberplate with the car's owner. It usually turned out to be a known associate of a trainer, and through this convoluted method the touts were almost always able to determine the dog's identity. The track touts were usually big punters, though two of the biggest over the years never attended trials. Blokes known only as Whispers and Michael Wales were greyhound owners who often plunged heavily on their own dogs. Michael once owned a stayer called Blue Mallee, which was in the kennels of a leading South Coast trainer. One night at Wentworth Park Michael's wife Trish, a primary school teacher, was regaling a group of us as to how she shopped at Franklins rather than Coles or Woolworths to save a few dollars on the weekly grocery bill. Her frugal habits were applauded by Michael, but poor Trish obviously had no idea how much money her husband was about to put on his dog.

A few minutes after Trish's treatise on budget shopping, Michael called me and Gary Manning aside to seek our assistance. 'Can you fellows help me put some money on Blue Mallee?' he asked. 'I'm having $10,000 on him.' As Blue Mallee was a notoriously slow starter, Gary and I thought Michael was letting his ownership of the dog affect his judgment. When we pointed this out to him, he replied: 'No, the trainer says Blue Mallee will go straight to the lead tonight.'

Gary and I muttered words to the effect of 'the trainer's kidding', but sure enough, when the boxes opened, Blue Mallee, with Michael's $10,000 on board, rocketed to the front and never looked like losing. Many years later his trainer was disqualified over a go-fast doping incident. So maybe Blue Mallee had a bit of help that night at Wenty.

Naturally everyone loves to get a bit of an edge when punting. That's human nature. Peter Davis, a mate of mine who these days works for the *Illawarra Mercury*, certainly did one night when he drove his pal Tony 'Plugger' Lockett, the AFL star, to hospital. It was a Friday night and Plugger, who was in agony, was diagnosed with appendicitis and admitted forthwith.

Quick as a flash Peter realised that Plugger's team, the Sydney Swans, were hot favourites to win their Aussie Rules match the following day. But without their star player they would do it tough. Realising there was no way Plugger would be on the field, Peter jumped on the phone and plunged heavily on the Swans' opponents, Geelong, at big odds. Insider trading? Sure. But there's no law against it. However, this time the bookmakers' guardian angel almost prevailed, with the Swans almost but not quite winning despite the absence of their champion point scorer. Peter was rewarded for his good deed in driving Plugger to hospital with a nice win on the punt!

When my wife-to-be Catherine arrived in Australia from France in 1973, I took her to the dogs. Noticing Whispers in a rather well-worn overcoat and shoes that had seen better days, she remarked: 'Oh, that poor gentleman seems down on his luck.' This of course was the European perception of wealth. There, if you have money, you always LOOK as if you have it. Australians, in the past especially, have tended to be ambivalent about their fortunes, as Catherine was soon to discover.

'Do you think he looks poor?' I asked Catherine. 'Look, he's going over to have a bet, let's follow him and see how much he puts on.' Catherine could hardly believe her ears when she heard Whispers place $5000 on the favourite. 'If he can afford to bet like that, why does he dress so modestly?' she inquired. I explained that to a lot of racegoers, punting is the prime focus of their life, so the way they dress matters little to them.

I had met Catherine on a 10,000 mile blind date in 1972. And I can thank the punt and rugby league for finding her. In late 1971 I was going pretty well on the punt and Bill Mordey suggested I join him when he headed to France the following year to cover the rugby league World Cup for the *Mirror*. I'd never been out of Australia and had no desire to travel overseas. But Bluegum Mordey was persuasive, pointing out, quite rightly, that if I didn't spend my punting winnings on a good trip I'd only lose it back to the bookies. So in 1972 off I went, planning to visit Ireland, which is the spiritual home of greyhound racing, and England, en route to France.

Bluegum booked me into the same French hotels in which he, the *Sun*'s Ernie Christensen and the *Sydney Morning Herald*'s Alan Clarkson were accommodated, along with the Australian team. Fate is a funny thing. The night before my plane left Sydney I attended a greyhound function and bumped into Charles 'Buck' Buchanan, a wealthy racehorse and greyhound owner who had contacts in Ireland and had occasionally imported dogs from there. Buck thrust a bundle of Irish greyhound newspapers into my hand, saying: 'There's some reading material for the plane trip. And I have organised for a mate of mine called Tommy Unwin to meet your flight in London. There's his phone number but he'll be there and he'll take care of you.'

With that he strode off. It was then I noticed, scrawled in ink on the top of the one of the Irish newspapers, 'CAR-3256'. I ran after Buck, asking him what the significance of this number was. 'Jesus,' he exclaimed. 'I forgot to tell you about that. It's the phone number of a girl in Paris who will show you the sights when you get to France. It can be a bastard of a place if you don't know anyone there.'

Of course, that girl in Paris turned out to be Catherine, my wife of 31 years and the mother of our four kids. But first I lobbed in London. There was nobody to meet me so I called the number Buck had supplied. The fellow with the broad English accent who answered the phone knew nothing about anyone called Jeff Collerson. But when I went to hang up, he said: 'Wait a minute, where are you from? You sound Australian.'

I told him that I was and explained I was a friend of Buck Buchanan's. 'Oh he's always been a slack letter writer,' said the voice, which turned out to belong to Tommy Unwin. 'Obviously he intended to write to me about you and has forgotten. Don't worry, I'll send my driver to Heathrow to collect you. You can stay with my wife Dot and I while you're in England.'

JEFF COLLERSON

Within an hour a chauffeur in a dark grey Rolls-Royce had collected the wide-eyed 27-year-old from Down Under. Off we headed to the Unwins' mansion in Roydon, near Essex, and the fun was about to begin. Tom Unwin was a builder who raced a team of greyhounds as a hobby. The hospitality he and his wife bestowed on an unknown young bloke from thousands of miles away was breathtaking.

One morning at breakfast they inquired if I liked the theatre. When I replied that my father had once taken me to the old Elizabethan Theatre at Newtown to see Robert Morley — an English character actor who later found fame doing advertisements for Heinz baked beans — Tom suggested we see some West End shows together.

I was boggle eyed as I scanned the theatre listings and discovered names like Deborah Kerr, Sir John Gielgud, Sir Ralph Richardson, Alan Bates and Milo O'Shea. But while Tom was a devotee of the theatre, he was also a larrikin. He announced one day that he was taking me to his club for lunch. 'You'll like that, luv,' said Dot. Boy, was that an understatement.

Tom's club was the Wigmore, a flash but somewhat infamous establishment where the father of Sarah Ferguson, the Duchess of York, found himself in trouble many years later. A photograph of Major Ferguson leaving the Wigmore Club made the front pages of the London tabloids. The reason was that while the Wigmore Club had everything something like Sydney's Tattersall's Club had as far as restaurants and facilities go, it trumped Australia's establishments in one respect. The pool/gymnasium area had individual spa baths and massage rooms staffed exclusively by stunning-looking Thai masseuses. The Thai ladies bathed, massaged and did just about anything to make club members happy, so my introduction to London club life was indeed memorable. As we left the club, following an excellent massage, spa and lunch, Tom asked me what I thought of the Wigmore Club. 'It blows City Tatt's out of the water,' I said.

After England I landed in Ireland, making my base in Limerick,

64

the home of the Irish Greyhound Board. I had never seen live-hare coursing, which had been long banned in Australia, so Des Hanrahan, the chairman of the Irish Board, offered to take me to a meeting at Loughrea, deep in the south. As we were tootling through the countryside, Des asked me my religion.

We were in what seemed a pretty remote place so I was tempted to lie. But having been brought up to tell the truth I told him I was a Protestant. Des had concern etched all over his face and said: 'Look, I said to my wife last night that coming from Australia there's every chance you'll turn out to be a Protestant. I've been churning about this ever since we've organised this trip, but I just had to ask you.'

I was completely baffled. While we were in the heart of Roman Catholic Ireland, I couldn't see what difference religion made to a visit to a greyhound coursing meeting. 'The problem is,' said Des, 'the food at the coursing is pretty dire. But we could have a grand lunch at the monastery at Loughrea, where my sister is the Mother Superior. I'll fully understand though if you have objections, on religious grounds, to eating in a monastery.'

I was gobsmacked. 'Des, you're kidding aren't you?' I said. 'I'll go anywhere for a feed!' Catholic Des was relieved and surprised, as it was obvious that he would not have expected his Protestant compatriots in the north of Ireland to join him for lunch in a monastery. Of course the monastery lunch, surrounded by nuns asking me questions like 'Do you ride kangaroos to work in Australia?', was a highlight of the trip.

Few hares were killed during the two-day coursing meeting. They were well fed and judiciously trained, with each hare seeming to know the precise location of the 'escape' at the end of the huge paddock in which the events were held. At coursing meetings dogs compete against each other in match-race situations. It is a knock-out contest, with the two undefeated hounds meeting in the final. At Loughrea this was the famous Connaught Cup. A judge, on horseback, decided the winner of each course by awarding the dogs points for speed and for forcing their quarry to turn sharply.

7

When They Smashed Every Plate at Souths Juniors

Irish hospitality is legendary, and when I arrived at Limerick I was collected by a local bookmaker. From Australia, Buck Buchanan had booked me into a flash hotel, the Inter-Continental, near Shannon Airport. But it was a little too pricey for me, so after one night there I asked the bookie if he could find alternative accommodation for the rest of my stay. He did, and I moved into a quaint old pub called Hanratty's Hotel, just off Henry Street, the main drag in Limerick, for a tariff of only £2 per night. After I'd settled in the bookie contacted me to say he had found an even cheaper place that was just £1 per night.

But by then I had unpacked, and liked the look of Hanratty's, so I stayed there. My first visit to Limerick greyhound races was an eye-opener. Greyhound racing in Ireland is run along similar lines to Australia, with virtually anyone able to secure a training licence and permitted to train a dog from their own residence. In England, however, professional trainers have kennels within the grounds of the different tracks. Owners must have their dogs with these trainers and can only see their dogs at certain times.

The big difference between Ireland and Australia was in the betting. Here, punters begin wagering as soon as the bookies put up their prices. But in Ireland few were interested in having a bet until the dogs came out onto the track for their pre-race parade. Irish punters like to have a good look at the dogs before they bet — here they are only concerned with what's in the form guide.

Because the Irish do their wagering in the final five minutes before the start of a race, the bookies at Limerick didn't have time to give change. I had £6 to 4 about a dog and gave the bookie five quid. I was waiting for my change when he turned to me and said: 'You'll get your change after the race, the same as everybody else.' After the race it was a real bun fight, with not only those who had backed the winner lining up to collect, but also those who had to get change from losing bets. It could only happen in Ireland.

Before I had left Australia Wally Dean, then manager of the plush and highly successful South Sydney Junior Leagues Club, and his mate Graham 'Croc' Palmer, who had a greyhound stud farm at Leppington, near Liverpool, Sydney, had asked me to obtain an Irish greyhound to stand at stud in Australia. Ireland is the recognised home of greyhound racing and in the early 1970s their stock had the reputation of being the best in the world.

I had got to know Croc through attending his two-up game near Parramatta railway station on the way home from Richmond dogs every Friday night. Although illegal, as every casino was in those days, Croc's Parramatta game was extremely well run. One night I saw a fellow win several thousand dollars and leave. A minute or so later another patron started to head out the door, only to have his way barred by the formidable personage of the Croc. 'You have to wait 10 minutes,' Croc told the patron. 'It's a security measure, mate, no offence intended. Anyone who has a big win is given plenty of time to get out of the area.'

My mate Bill Mordey would have been the most fearless gambler at Croc's two-up. I've seen Bluegum turn $100 into $5000 and then finish up having to snip Croc for the taxi fare to get home by the time the game closed. Croc, who used to say he got his nickname after biting off a gangster's ear in a brawl, wanted to stand an Irish import at his VIP Kennels. He had formed a partnership with Wally Dean and Bill Mordey to buy such a stud dog. I was asked to use my contacts in Ireland to ensure they got the right animal, and for my expertise and troubles I was to be given a quarter share in the hound.

Pat Holland, then secretary of the Bord na gCon — the Irish Greyhound Board — helped me find a dog called Super Approval. When the dog arrived in Australia he caused a sensation, but not because he was the best performed stud dog ever imported to this part of the world. Wally Dean arranged a civic reception for the greyhound in the banquet room of Souths Juniors, and invitations were dispatched to all the top sports columnists, including the *Sydney Morning Herald*'s Rod Humphries and the *Daily Telegraph*'s Mike Gibson.

Guests — including Super Approval, who was seated at the official table — feasted on lobster and rare roast beef. We even managed to get some photographs published in the Sydney dailies and the high-circulation Melbourne sports weekly the *Sporting Globe*, of Super Approval sipping 'wine' (it was actually water) from a crystal goblet. But when those photos were published all hell broke loose.

While it had the desired effect of making Super Approval the most publicised greyhound ever to arrive in Australia, it caused outrage among a few Souths Juniors club members. A couple of them contacted the NSW Health Department complaining about a dog licking food off a plate and drinking out of a wine glass in their banquet room. The result? Souths Juniors had to smash every plate and glass used at the function. But while finding Super Approval in Ireland was fun, my real coup from there was phoning, from my room at Hanratty's, the French girl Buck Buchanan had teed up for me.

Buck had been at pains to impress upon me that he had guaranteed me to her. But I wasn't sure whether I was guaranteed to be a gentleman or a stud proposition. It turned out to be the former, and when I lobbed in France, Catherine Vivien was at

Orly Airport to meet me. Here was this attractive 20-year-old, who was attending the Sorbonne, yet who was apparently a close friend of Buck Buchanan's, a bloke in his sixties. I was puzzled but it turned out that Catherine's brother Patrick lived in Melbourne and was married to Buck's daughter Karen.

Catherine and I hit it off immediately and I invited her to the Lido the day after I arrived. A Sydney greyhounds bookmaker, Neville Mogler, who had travelled the world and wined and dined in all the best places, had told me not to miss the Lido, declaring it the most spectacular nightclub he had seen. It lived up to expectations. It was expensive, even back in 1972 costing something like $100 per person which included only a half bottle of Champagne. But it was worth every cent.

For the opening act they lowered onto the stage a huge tank of water which was occupied by topless 'mermaids' performing a spectacular underwater ballet. When that concluded, the tank was removed, the lights dimmed, and a few minutes later the stage became a re-creation of the Louvre. A couple of masked bandits were in the process of stealing the 'Mona Lisa', and were scooped up by a real helicopter, which suddenly flew over the heads of the audience. No sooner had the thieves climbed into their helicopter than a police helicopter arrived and a gun battle ensured over our heads. All this in a nightclub!

After intermission, out came a trio of spectacularly dressed, pre-French Revolution characters on horseback, who began to ride their charges towards the audience. The horses were on a conveyor belt-type treadmill, which went faster as they picked up speed. As we left the Lido, I asked Catherine if she went there often. 'I've never been before,' she said. 'I can't afford places like that, they are for rich tourists.'

Next morning, over breakfast at Paris' Hotel Lutetia, Bill Mordey asked me how the date with 'the Froggy sheila' went. I replied: 'Terrific. I think I'm sweet there. The Lido was sensational. I'm taking her out again tonight but I don't know how I can come up with something to match last night.' Said Mordey:

'Leave it to me. The Crazy Horse Saloon is on a par with the Lido, but you must get the special seats there. Let me book them for you.'

That night Catherine and I filed into the Crazy Horse Saloon, which was similar in design and style to the Lido. Couples sat at tables scattered around the club, but when I showed the maitre d' the tickets Bill had organised for us he took Catherine and me down to a long bench just below the front of the stage. 'There must be some mistake,' I said, 'these seats look awful.' Reassured these were indeed the seats I had paid for, Catherine and I took our places alongside a row of desperate-looking male characters.

We had to look upwards to see the stage but before I could complain further the lights dimmed and the show began. Out came a long chorus line of beautiful female dancers, who opened their act with a rousing rendition of the French can-can. As they began their high-stepping, high-kicking routine, all I could see was a line of pubic hair. None of the chorus line was wearing knickers! It then dawned on me that Catherine and I had tickets to the perverts' row.

Catherine was the only female on the long bench and I realised this was my mate Bluegum's idea of a great joke. '*Pardonnez moi, c'est mon ami* Mordey's warped sense of humour,' I blathered to Catherine. 'Don't worry, I am broad-minded,' she reassured me. Of course the next morning, as I came down the stairs to the breakfast room at the Lutetia, a grinning Mordey yelled out: 'How were those seats I got you at the Crazy Horse, mate!' 'You bludger,' I replied, 'it's a wonder Catherine is still speaking to me. She must think I'm the worst pervert in the world.'

But once she had met Mordey, Catherine realised what a prankster he was and we all had a good laugh about the knicker-less dancers. Catherine made some sort of history a few nights later when she became the first French woman to ride in the Australian rugby league team bus while the players were on their way to play France. It happened like this.

The Aussies were set to take on France in a World Cup at the luxurious Paris stadium, Le Parc des Princes, and were meeting in the foyer of the Hotel Lutetia. I was set to travel with them in the team bus along with the Australian coach Harry Bath and Bill Mordey, Ernie Christensen and Alan Clarkson. Catherine was about to see her first rugby league game, and as I knew there would be plenty of room I asked her to meet us at the Lutetia and hop on the bus.

But Clancy Kingston, the team manager, was horrified at this idea. 'No way,' he said. 'This tour is already turning into a bloody circus and as we're going to play France there's no way we're having a Froggy sheila on the bus with us.' But poor old Clancy got howled down. Team members including John 'Lurch' O'Neill, along with my old schoolmate Freddy Jones and Bobby 'Bozo' Fulton began giving it to Clancy. 'Don't be a nark,' yelled Lurch. 'Let Jeff bring his French sheila on the bus.' Added Freddy: 'You're kidding, Clancy. What harm is that going to do? Be a good sport.'

Much to Catherine's embarrassment, Clancy relented, and on we piled into a seat behind Arthur 'Big Artie' Beetson and Bob 'the Bear' O'Reilly. The trip to the ground seated behind a couple of typically Aussie footballing rough 'n' tumble characters like Artie and the Bear really gave Catherine an introductory shot of Australian culture! But the team was on its best behaviour, with someone calling out as the bus took off: 'No swearing, boys. There's a sheila on the bus and she's a Frog!'

As expected, Australia flogged France, a nation where soccer and rugby union are far more popular and where league had been in decline since its glory days of the 1950s. In the final Australia finished up beating a strong English team which included several outstanding players who later played in the Sydney first-grade competition. Although I had not yet begun writing a wine column for News Limited — that began 16 years later — the trip to France furthered my interest in wine.

Catherine's dad Robert was, like most Frenchmen, keen on wine, although only inasmuch as he treated it as a simple beverage and a component of all meals. Like many Parisian office workers, Robert would come home for a hot lunch every day.

His wife Marcelline, wherever she was in the morning, used to dash home around 11.30 to prepare his meal. And that meal always included at least a half-bottle of red wine, after which Robert would head back to the office.

Years later an Australian winemaker friend of mine landed the job managing Hardys Wines' La Baume Winery at Poitiers, in the south of France. He was horrified when, during his first day on the new job, everyone, from the office workers to his fellow winemakers and grape pickers and growers, downed tools promptly at noon. 'The biggest traffic jam in Poitiers was when the whole town headed home for lunch every day,' he later recalled.

'That first day at La Baume, our chief accountant disappeared at noon and didn't get back until after three o'clock. I was about to remonstrate with him when I was advised not to attempt to change the way things were done. They'd been working this way for a hundred years, so for an interloper from Australia to interfere would have caused a rebellion. So I bit my tongue and later had to admit that the accountant worked through until seven o'clock at night. So the work got done, they just did it differently and over a longer time span than in Australia.'

There was no sniffing, slurping and spitting with Catherine's father and, typical of a French consumer, he knew little about grape varieties. He referred to his nation's wines by their regional name, not the grape, preferred Bordeaux to Burgundy, favoured Henriot above other Champagnes, and used Chinon, a medium-bodied tipple from the Loire Valley, as his house red. When he gave me a welcoming glass of Chinon, I asked him what was the grape variety. He looked nonplussed, simply replying: '*C'est Chinon*' (It's Chinon). I later discovered Chinon was made from 100 per cent cabernet franc. Bob and his wife Marcelline trusted me enough to let me take their daughter to the wine regions of Alsace and Macon for a few days of wine tasting and I have them to thank for boosting my passion for wine — and for their daughter.

After leaving France at the end of the 1972 World Cup I

corresponded with Catherine for 12 months. My dear old naive mum, who, confusedly, thought lesbians came from Lebanon, used to phone me at work with the news: 'A new French letter has just arrived for you!' For her 21st birthday Catherine's parents gave her a ticket to Australia, the plan being to see if we were still fond enough of each other to continue our relationship. She arrived on Good Friday, 1973.

Our rekindled romance got off to a rocky start when my Holden Torana broke down on the way to my parents' Frenchs Forest home from the airport. But I made up for it when I took Catherine to the Royal Easter Show on Easter Saturday — she thought the wood-chopping was sensational. That night she accompanied me to Wentworth Park dogs and the following day I ferried her off to Brookvale Oval to watch Manly-Warringah's three rugby league games, first-, reserve- and third-grade. Just to really spoil her I dragged her along to the qualifying trials at Harold Park dogs 24 hours later! There were 108 heats, with Ray Hadley, now one of radio's biggest stars, the race caller. How's that for a welcome-to-Australia baptism of fire?

Catherine and I began renting a flat at Kirribilli, which had its own wharf. One morning we were sitting in the sun when she noticed a stack of mussels clinging to the pylons on the little marina. 'Let's have mussels for dinner,' the little Parisienne exclaimed excitedly. 'Hang on,' I exclaimed. 'There are sharks in Sydney Harbour and anyhow, it's probably too polluted to be eating mussels from here.' But Catherine, with typical Gallic stubbornness, insisted on diving in and, armed with a bucket and a knife, procured around three dozen molluscs which made a fabulous feast that night for dinner.

I also introduced Catherine to the world of Sydney's illegal, but widely tolerated, casinos. A bookmaker friend, Peter McCullen, had a roulette system but needed two other people to help him operate it. He recruited Catherine and me and we were soon regulars at George Walker's Goulburn Club, above the old Chequers nightclub in the CBD's Goulburn Street, at the Forbes

Club in Woolloomooloo, at Joe Taylor's Palace Club at Kings Cross and at a casino above the Telford Arcade in Bondi Junction.

Peter's system was based on a staking plan. We would watch the first roulette wheel spin, and if it had come down as, say, number one red, we would then have $2 on black, $2 on an even number, and $2 on a high number. If the next spin produced number five red, we would double each of our bets. We would continue doing this until we got a favourable result, after which we would revert to a $2 bet on the opposite number or colour to what had just come up. It was a lot of fun and at the end of a year we split a modest profit.

The current legal, huge and glitzy casinos leave me cold. They don't have the atmosphere of places like the Goulburn Club, which were shut when casinos became legal. The small, intimate setting of the Goulburn Club included free toasted sandwiches and drinks for its patrons, served by stunning-looking young women sporting plunging necklines. They would use their physical assets to the club's advantage too. On one occasion I was backing the colours while Catherine backed odds and evens and Peter put our money on the high and low numbers.

I was due to put $256 on red when a knockout blonde leaned over me, pushed her breasts in my face, and asked if I wanted a drink. While I was chatting to — and staring at — her, the croupier sang out the familiar 'no more bets please' and I didn't get my bet on. Peter was fuming, as was Catherine, and I'm sure it had been a none-too-subtle ruse by the club management to thwart our system. I've often joked that after that first week here Catherine must have said to herself, 'How long has this been going on?' and vowed never to return to France.

During my first trip to France in 1972 I became friends with Lurch O'Neill. Like a lot of footballers who are renowned for their rough 'n' tumble ways on the field, Lurch was as kind as a kitten away from the game and a man of great principle. A few years after getting back from France, I hadn't seen Lurch for a while and bumped into his former South Sydney and Australian team-mate Gary Stevens. Gary and Lurch were partners in a building business and Gary was doing some renovation work at News Limited's Surry Hills offices.

When I asked him how Lurch was, Gary replied: 'Same as always, worrying all the time.' This astounded me because Lurch had always seemed like the type of guy who wouldn't stress about anything at all. When I asked Gary to elaborate he said: 'Mate, Lurch is the world's greatest worrier. But it has worked in our favour in this business.'

Gary then explained that for their first News Limited job they were to be paid something like $10,000, but due to a mix-up in the accounts department they were sent a cheque for a substantially larger sum. When this happened Lurch was beside himself with worry, and despite several anxious phone calls to the various News Limited departments was told they had been paid the correct amount. Now a lot of people might have taken the money and run, but not Lurch. He was worried sick. In desperation, he trudged into News Limited and knocked on the door of Brian Hogben.

Hogben was one of Rupert Murdoch's right-hand men and was amazed when Lurch handed the incorrect cheque back to him. 'Look, we need the $10,000 desperately, so can you cancel this cheque and organise for us to get the right amount?' the footballer said. Hogben, his faith in human nature restored, commented to Lurch that he was surprised there were such honest people left in the world. 'As far as I am concerned, Stevens and O'Neill will do all News Limited's building works from now on.' Hogben was true to his word, and when News Limited undertook huge refurbishing of its offices a couple of years ago the work was done by the Stevens and O'Neill building company. Tragically John O'Neill died of cancer a few years back. It surprised nobody that his funeral service had St Mary's Cathedral, in the heart of Sydney, filled to overflowing.

8

Australia's Biggest Dog Punter

Bookmakers are an often unfairly maligned group. Maybe I'm a dinosaur, but I reckon it will be a sad day when, through natural attrition, they disappear from Australian racetracks. I think the tendency by punters to rubbish bookies is because when they back a loser, they can hardly vent their frustration or anger on an on-course totalisator or off-course TAB machine. But the human being with the bag around his neck at the races is fair game.

At the greyhounds, the halcyon times when there were 150 bookmakers at Wentworth Park have long gone. These days there are no more than five bookies competing with the TAB/tote giant. At Wentworth Park John Stollery, who bets on the interstate meetings, and Don Bowron, who until late 2004 operated a multiple doubles book there, have between them had bookies' licences for over a century.

Stollery made history on 18 December 1989 when he laid the biggest single bet ever recorded on a greyhound track in Australia. A woman punter placed $202,000 on a dog with the unlikely name of True Blue Tah at odds of 2/1 on. When True Blue Tah won, she picked up $101,000, in effect, giving her a profit for her night's work at Wentworth Park of $14,000, as I'll explain later. My story on the mystery woman's betting activities made the front page of the *Daily Mirror* the next day. It was one of the few times the dogs had made the hallowed front page — another occasion being in the

1970s when Hec Watt, owner-trainer of the great Zoom Top, forgot to remove a raincoat from the champ before boxing her for a big race at Goulburn.

Naturally, Zoom Top, the long odds-on favourite, was beaten and Watt was barred from handling her in future events. There was never any question of ill intent by Watt — who loved to see Zoom Top win — but he had not been well and was getting on in years, and simply forgot to remove the plastic rug covering his star.

But back to Stollery's big bet. The woman, a bespectacled, slightly built lady who wore a veil and was always accompanied by a burly bodyguard, caused much excitement on Sydney greyhound tracks in the late 1980s. Her tactic was simple. She backed the first favourite to win $14,000. If it won she left the track. If it was beaten, she would back the second favourite to win what she had lost on the first race, plus her $14,000 race-night goal. Her theory was that while a horse race meeting often went by without a favourite being successful, it seldom happened at the dogs. She apparently had unlimited money and in Stollery she found the only bookie willing to accept such massive wagering. On 18 December the mystery woman lost $25,000 on an odds-on chance called Cee Me Ezy in the first race, while endeavouring to win $14,000. In race two she put $26,000 on Mac's Little Mate, which also lost, and she then splurged $36,000 on Class Captain in race three, which was another loser. But True Blue Tah won race four, recouping all the woman's losses for the night plus her $14,000 target.

Ironically, favourites won the next four events. 'But had True Blue Tah lost, she would have had to put an unbelievable amount of money on Farrarami, winner of race five, because that greyhound was odds-on too,' Stollery said later. But of course, the inevitable happened. On 8 January 1990, not a single favourite won at Wentworth Park and after losing $200,000 the mystery woman, who had always been known only as Val, fled the course and was never seen on a racetrack again.

Retired not too long ago were Tony McInerney and Peter McCullen, who are a long way removed from the Hollywood movie image of what a bookmaker is supposed to be like. When he retired from bookmaking McInerney devoted his life to charity work, putting in endless hours volunteering at the Matthew Talbot Hostel and at St Vincent de Paul stores.

Now he makes regular visits to long-term prisoners, usually lifers who get no other visitors and so have no contact with the outside world. Tony told me: 'They are usually people who have committed horrendous crimes, like murdering children.' When I asked him how he could bring himself to visit creatures like this, he replied simply: 'It's not up to me to judge them. That's for God to decide.'

Not long after moving into a retirement village in north-west Sydney, Peter McCullen called me to say he now had a paper run. He explained: 'The newspapers are dumped in a bundle next to the main gate but most of the old people here can't get around well enough to fetch theirs. So I gather them up and distribute one to each unit.'

McCullen was not only a leading bookmaker, but at one stage owned the greatest stud dog ever imported from overseas. Waverly Supreme earned something in the vicinity of $500,000 during his career. Yet McCullen secured him through a fluke.

'I was in Dublin in 1971 and went to the dogs,' McCullen explained. 'I noticed a fellow and his daughter who each had four greyhounds on leads. Wanting to have a bet and not knowing the local form, I asked this chap to mark my racebook. He turned out to be Gay McKenna, who, along with his brother Ger, were Ireland's leading trainers. Anyway Gay tipped me a few winners so I gave him £20 as a present. The next time I went to the dogs in Dublin Gay was waiting for me, keen to mark my book again. He tipped more winners and this time got a 50 quid sling. I gave him my home phone number in Australia, telling him that if ever he was in our part of the world to give me a call and I'd show him some hospitality.

'A year later he phoned me at two o'clock in the morning. He said he owned a fast dog called Waverly Supreme which could not race again, having just broken his leg in a race. Naturally I was half asleep, and in somewhat of a daze I agreed to buy the dog for $3500. I regretted it the next morning but I never go back on my word so the dog was soon on his way to Australia. Waverly Supreme began his stud career at a $200 service fee but was so successful he was soon commanding a $1000 fee. He was the first stud dog to earn a four figure amount for each bitch he served and was the top sire in Australia for eight years.'

The late Freddy Stapleton began his bookmaking career at Lithgow dogs in the early 1950s. Freddy saved a bank for his first meeting, something like £1000. But when he got to Lithgow he was mortified to find the grass track covered in snow and ice. The club secretary announced that the meeting would have to be abandoned unless some volunteers could be found who were willing to shovel and sweep the icy debris from the course. There were no takers initially, but Freddy, chomping at the bit to begin his bookmaking career, managed to persuade a half dozen dog trainers to help him. After 45 minutes toiling away in the bitter cold, Freddy and his working party had the track ready for racing.

Freddy most likely regretted his efforts because after 10 races he was flat broke. Freddy recovered, however, and like most bookies he was extremely generous. So many punters bet with him on the nod — that is, on credit — that he once had debts of around $400,000. And that was back in the 1970s!

In September 2004 a Wentworth Park bookie named Brendan McCoy caused a sensation, and was later reprimanded, when he dashed out onto the track near the finish of a race. A dog called Chief Tanga had turned around and run back towards the field as the dogs came into the straight. Chief Tanga looked set to disrupt the race when Brendan suddenly appeared on the scene to take control of the wayward dog. Everyone thought Brendan was doing this out of some sort of civic duty. But he later told me that Mint Secret, the dog which was leading at the time and would have lost had the event been declared a 'no race' by the stewards, was a huge result for him. 'Not a single person backed Mint Secret with me,'

Brendan explained. 'He was a skinner for me. So naturally I didn't want anything untoward to happen with the result.' Unfortunately for Brendan his athletic performance was in vain, as the stewards decided Chief Tanga's reverse running had affected the minor placings.

In the mid-1980s I launched a successful betting plunge at Mudgee dogs, betting with bookmakers Max Hallinan and Bob McLoughan, two good blokes. Gary Manning and I part-owned a greyhound called Tivoli Bonnara who had won a couple of races in the city in 1984 and had been retired. She had whelped a litter of pups but her trainer Charlie Gatt had put her back into training. Tivoli Bonnara — her kennel name was Rachel — began trialling well and Charlie decided to set her for a race at Mudgee.

Tivoli Bonnara had always raced under my mother's maiden name, so appeared in the racebook as owned by Miss Emily Booth. Anyhow Gary wasn't interested in making the long trip to Mudgee and told me he didn't want to back his greyhound. Knowing he was very close to Max Hallinan, one of only two bookmakers operating at Mudgee, I asked Gary to say nothing about how well the old stager was going. But Gary, who has always been an extremely loyal bloke, replied: 'I can't do that, mate. Max is too good a friend, I'll have to tell him she is flying.'

Just as I was pondering if there was any point in me going to Mudgee under those circumstances, Gary seemed to read my mind. 'Don't worry,' he said. 'Max will still bet you. He gambles against the Sydney dogs every week and over the years reckons he is a long way in front.'

Gary arranged for me to meet Max in the car park before the meeting. Max asked me what price I was after and I said I thought 5/2 ($3.50 in today's parlance) was fair. I told him I wanted to put $1500 on Tivoli Bonnara so he offered to bet me $1500 to $600 then and there. 'I always put my prices up first and whatever I display, Bob McLoughan will copy,' said Max. 'So you put yourself in front of Bob's stand and you'll get $1500 to $600 with him too.

The other $300 you'll have to put on with him at reduced odds. Is that okay?'

I agreed and Max then introduced me to Bob McLoughan, who at that time was a part-owner of the champion race dog Brother Fox. Bob asked me what I was doing at Mudgee, and not wanting to alert him that there was a plunge in the offing I told him I been touring the local vineyards and decided to call in at the dogs on the way home. Bob offered to bet me a point over the odds on anything I wanted to back. I had a couple of $10 bets as burley and then came Tivoli Bonnara's race. Sure enough Max Hallinan opened her at 5/2 while I positioned myself in front of Bob's stand. Right on cue he copied Max's price and I claimed him $1500 to $600. Bob was taken aback but set me. 'How come you're having so much on this dog?' he asked.

I explained I had been following her career and he wound the price down to 2/1. I put the other $300 on her at those odds and Tivoli Bonnara, bless her little heart and soul, won by a nose.

The following day Ronnie Brown, a Sydney trainer who was a friend of McLoughan's, phoned the Mudgee bookie to inquire as to how he had fared the previous night. Bob lamented: 'That bloke Jeff Collerson was touring the vineyards and put $900 on a dog which won. He completely ruined my night.' Brownie asked the name of the dog and when Bob told him he roared laughing down the phone. 'No wonder he backed it, he owns it!' he said. Although Brownie effectively shelved me, the next time I saw Bob McLoughan he bore no grudges and even asked if Tivoli Bonnara was still racing.

They say that most owners let their hearts rule their heads when they bet, but not Gary Manning. While he did back Tivoli Bonnara in some of her wins, he put $3000 on her rival one night at Harold Park. Billy Fletcher, a crack trainer of stayers, had a dog in a 732-metre race called Powerful World, which Gary declared a special. Before the race Tivoli Bonnara's trainer Charlie Gatt told me to advise Gary to save on her, saying she was very fit and had a chance at long odds of toppling Powerful

World. I had $50 on Tivoli Bonnara at 10/1 but Gary ignored his trainer's tip and plunged only on Powerful World.

Tivoli Bonnara went straight to the lead and although getting tired in the straight, just lasted to beat the fast-finishing Powerful World, who was notoriously slow early. I'd been cheering her by her kennel name — 'Go Rachel, go Rachel' — in Gary's ear all the way down the straight. So when they crossed the line he yelled at me: 'Pigeon, you know what you can do with Rachel! Just get down to the secretary's office and pick up my share of the prize-money.' It was the only time Gary ever insisted on getting his portion of the stakes. On all the other occasions when Tivoli Bonnara won, he was happy just to back her.

Of course in the old days, when some country tracks drew 400 entries for a 10-race program which could accommodate only 100 dogs, it was not uncommon for a trainer or owner to leave the prizemoney behind. One Saturday afternoon a trainer I was involved with won a treble, one of which was a dog I owned. It was my chore, while the trainer was loading the dogs into the trailer to head home, to sign for the prizemoney. 'But don't take it,' the trainer said. 'We've had a good day on the punt and if we don't leave the prizemoney we might not get a start next week.' There were stories of secretary/graders owning mansions thanks to forfeited prizemoney, but I never saw any evidence of this.

People often ask me if I have finished in front in my 40 years punting on the pooches. I've never kept records but I do know that tipping a winner helped me move from being a cadet to a graded journalist. When I came to News Limited as a cadet journo in 1968, we had a shorthand teacher called Miss Kirsop. Nobody could complete their cadetship, and thus become a fully fledged D-grade journalist, without being able to write shorthand at 120 words per minute.

I was not too flash at shorthand but dear old Miss Kirsop was a keen punter. In the late 1960s I used to enjoy a bet on the horses too and tipped Miss Kirsop a neddy called Ramsay. The horse duly won and Miss Kirsop picked up enough cash to buy a new stopwatch, which she needed to time her shorthand classes. She nicknamed the timepiece Ramsay, and in the shorthand exam, when I couldn't quite manage the 120 wpm, Miss Kirsop still gave me a big tick and a pass — thanks to that winning tip.

Like bookmakers, punters are a rare breed. Usually they are the most generous people on earth, probably because money gets to an 'easy come, easy go' stage with them. A lot of punters like to put aside a secret bank which they can call on for a rainy day. Tony Zuccarini, who these days puts the *Sydney Morning Herald* racing formguide together, is such a punter.

A few years back, living with his parents in Sydney's west, Zooky had $3000 stashed away in the pocket of an old checked shirt in his wardrobe. One night he returned from a late shift at work and was horrified to discover the shirt was gone. His mum explained that she had cleared out all the wardrobes and put what she deemed as surplus clothes, including her son's shirt, in a charity bin a few streets away. Although it was midnight Zooky had no idea when the bin would be emptied so had to act fast. Now Tony at that time must have tipped the scales at around 150 kilograms, so there wasn't much hope of him being able to squeeze into the bin. Desperate, he phoned his sister Connie and asked her to get her nine-year-old son Gino out of bed. 'I've got a job for him,' explained Tony. 'Are you crazy?' said Connie 'He has to go to school tomorrow. I'm not waking him up at midnight.'

But when Zooky explained the urgent situation Connie agreed, and a few minutes later little Gino found himself, armed with a torch, being lowered into a charity bin. 'He was terrified but he found it God bless him,' Tony told me later. 'I gave him $20 for his trouble.' A light sling, Tony, a light sling.

Tony might have under-paid Gino on that occasion but I recall him queuing up for hours to buy rugby league grand final tickets for his nephew and there's no doubt he is one of the kindest people I've met. A couple of years back Richard Zammit, now president of the National Coursing Association, one of the two city greyhound clubs, Tony Zuccarini and I were chewing the fat in the press room at Wentworth Park. A well-known punter poked his head in the door and asked to see Richard privately. A few minutes later Richard returned, beaming. 'Gee that's a big result,' he said. 'That bloke has owed me $1500 for 12 months. I was ready to kiss it goodbye but he just paid me. He must have kicked a goal.'

Tony piped up: 'What about me, did he say he wanted to see me too?' explaining the same punter had owed him $2000 for 18 months. 'No, he didn't mention you,' said Richard. A philosophical Zooky took it like this: 'Oh well, maybe he owes a lot of people and is working his way through the alphabet.'

I guess it is the dream of all punters to be able to get a bet on when a race is over. That punting fantasy once came true for John Buttsworth, a dog trainer from Bathurst. But John got little out of the deal. It happened like this.

He was at Orange dogs one Saturday night and a bookmaker was betting on the Sydney greyhounds. This was in the pre-video, pre-televised racing days and John was listening to the Sydney meeting through 2KY on his transistor. He was astounded when he heard a race, and then noticed the bookie still offering 5/2 about the winner. John had no money with him, so grabbed a friend who had a dog engaged at Orange later in the night. 'How much money have you got?' John asked urgently. 'Two hundred bucks,' came the reply.

'Quick, go and put it on number four at Wentworth Park, it has just won,' said John. The punter appeared to get set just before a call came over the Orange racetrack loudspeakers. The call advised that the landline to Sydney had been lost and all betting was to cease. 'Did he bet you $500 to $200?' John asked his mate. 'He would have,' said his fellow trainer, 'but I only had $100 on the dog.'

John was incredulous. 'Why would you do that, knowing the dog had already won?' he said. 'Oh, I wanted to keep $100 to put on my own dog later tonight. I was worried you might have mis-heard the call.' Relating the story later, John lamented to me: 'Fair dinkum, you just can't help some people!'

Racetracks are never lacking in humorous characters, and George West, a fixture on Sydney greyhound tracks between the 1950s and 1980s, had some terrific expressions. Ask George how his luck was and you'd get the stock answer, 'Terrible, if it was raining movie stars I'd get Lassie.' Of a rude person George would remark, 'You say hello to him and he's stuck for an answer.' And if anyone was a nuisance, George was often heard to say: 'He's such a pest he'd give a Bex a headache' (Bex headache powders were a 1950s precursor to today's Panadol).

Another great character with a sense of humour is leading trainer Johnny Mooney. In late 2004 Johnny was telling me a tale about a dog and its trainer. 'Oh you must remember him, that little fawn dog trained by that skinny bloke,' he said. When I told Johnny I needed a bit more information than that, he racked his brain a while longer and couldn't come up with any answers. 'Mate, you'll have to forgive me. I have this rare medical condition,' he said, tapping his forehead. 'It's called craft.' I began sympathising with him but when I inquired what 'craft' was, Mooney said: 'Can't remember a fucking thing!'

9

Ring-in and Doping Scandals at the Dogs

Like all sports greyhound racing has had its share of doping scandals. The most recent occurred in April 2000 when the NSW Greyhound Racing Authority's chief steward, Rodney Potter, was caught tampering with urine samples taken from greyhounds. Potter became the central figure in an Independent Commission Against Corruption inquiry, chaired by Irene Moss. It was found he had taken bribes to either (a) not drug-test dogs from the kennels of certain trainers, or (b) dispose of any drug-tainted urine samples and replace them with clean samples before testing began. Potter was sacked and later jailed for his part in the affair, while three leading trainers — Ron Gill, Ken Howe and Ray King, along with one of the sport's most successful owners, Andy Sarcasmo — were disqualified for life.

But the biggest calamity to hit the sport in modern times came almost two decades ago. That's when the great ring-in scam was uncovered, a hoax which resulted in one of the sport's leading trainers, Jack Pringle, from Orange, being handed a permanent disqualification. Jack now regrets that he ever became involved in substituting top-grade dogs for lesser-performed animals. But he does have a touch of pride in recalling the comment of Ron Nicholas, the chief steward of the NSW Greyhound Racing

Control Board, who meted out the life term. In the *Greyhound Recorder* newspaper at the time of the ring-in saga, Nicholas conceded Pringle's scheme was 'ingenious'.

Jack told me recently that he came up with the substitution ploy after topping the Sydney trainers' premiership yet finishing square financially. 'I was often in a neck-and-neck struggle with Paul Cauchi, a leading Sydney trainer, to see who would take out the annual premiership. Just over 20 years ago I won a stack of races in the metropolitan area and on paper had my most successful year. Yet when I looked at my finances I had not shown a single dollar profit. Expenses of running the kennels, the breeding and rearing farms and operating vehicles to take the dogs all over Australia killed me. I decided there had to be another way and I came up with it.'

According to Jack, he once had 260 phantom greyhounds on his property. His modus operandi was this. He would borrow a nondescript brood bitch from a breeder and have her mated with a similarly unfashionable stud dog. After the mating had been registered with the authorities, Jack would abort the pregnancy. With an acquiescent marking steward on side, a phantom litter was registered and Jack would add four pups to an already genuine litter. 'At one stage I had 15 brood bitches on loan,' he recalls. 'In those days breeders were sent the registration papers before the pups were ear-branded, usually when they were a year old. Because of me they changed the system completely. Now pups are marked and ear-branded at three months.'

Jack Pringle's biggest win came at the Gabba, the famous Brisbane cricket ground which, up to the 1980s, was also the home of Queensland's main greyhound track. Today Pringle's home carries a cheeky plaque bearing the name Gabba Lodge. He says: 'I raced Temple Quest, who was one of Australia's best stayers, in a low-grade event at the Gabba under the name of Sister Illy. I probably won about $50,000 on her that night but that was when I came unstuck.

'Another leading trainer, who was from Sydney, happened to be at the Gabba when Sister Illy won. Temple Quest-cum-Sister Illy had an unusual galloping action and when this trainer next raced against me at Harold Park, I noticed him studying Temple Quest closely. He had a sharp eye because he detected the identical galloping styles of Temple Quest and Sister Illy, who of course were one and the same greyhound. Then at Harold Park, he noted that Temple Quest had precisely the same markings as the greyhound he had seen win in Brisbane under the name Sister Illy. He notified the authorities and after some detailed checking of ear-brands listed on the nomination forms of both greyhounds they were alerted. My place was raided around four o'clock in the morning and I was busted.'

Ken Norquay, a NSW greyhound racing official who helped coordinate the raid, told me at the time that Jack Pringle's comment was: 'What's the problem? I was only robbing bookmakers!'

Another big betting coup Jack landed during his ring-in routine was when a puppy called Brindle Bounce won a maiden race at Wangaratta in Victoria's north-east. Wangaratta, which raced on Friday nights in those days, had a strong betting ring. Among the resident bookmakers was Des Stone, who was later called to Sydney to testify against Pringle. After Brindle Bounce had landed a mammoth betting plunge winning a 400-metre maiden race at Wangaratta, Des phoned me in Sydney.

'Mate, I want you to look for a dog for me,' he yelled down the phone. 'Why, do you want to buy one?' I replied. 'No,' Des said. 'I want to back a dog called Brindle Bounce the next time it races. It's a champion and I want to be on it anywhere in Australia.' He explained that although Brindle Bounce had raced at Wangaratta under the ownership of an obscure character, he was convinced Jack Pringle was involved.

He said that the supposedly unraced dog, which had drawn box eight, was backed from 2/1 to 1/5 favouritism, and not only won by a dozen lengths but smashed the track record, a feat unheard of for an unraced puppy. 'There was a punter in front of each bookie's stand,' Des said. 'When betting commenced each punter would claim their bookie for $2000 to $1000, and then, as the price came down, would remain in place wanting to put more money on the dog. In the end some of these punters were wanting $10,000 on to win $2000, odds of 5/1 on! It was unbelievable.'

Of course I never found Brindle Bounce for Dessie, simply because the dog's real name was Run to Mummy. When Jack Pringle was charged over the affair I visited his kennels and he pointed out Run to Mummy to me. 'He was a pretty quick hound,' he said. Run to Mummy certainly was, but he had trouble running out a strong 457 metres at Harold Park, Sydney's main venue at that time. Run to Mummy, a wide runner who desperately wanted an outside box, took out a few races at Harold Park by setting up huge early leads and falling in to win. But once he reached top-grade he had trouble winning.

When Jack pointed the dog out to me, I naively remarked: 'Gee, you'd have got some money out of him if he had been able to run a strong 457 metres.' To which Jack replied: 'Yeah, but I did get a few dollars out of him one night at Wangaratta when I ran him in a 400-metre maiden under the name Brindle Bounce!' Little wonder Jack's punters were keen to lay the long odds-on about a top Sydney dog who was not only perfectly boxed and racing over his pet distance, but was contesting a maiden event at humble Wangaratta.

Not that all of Jack's plunges came off. He prepared Temple Quest's litter brother Prince Regis for a 700-metre event at the Gabba, which seemed to be Jack's favourite haunt. Prince Regis needed to have reasonable form in order to secure a start at the principal Queensland course, so Jack ran the dog, a dyed-in-the-wool stayer, in a couple of unsuitable 400-metre races in the bush. Everything went perfectly when Prince Regis, unbacked in the two bush events, won both but in very slow times. Those wins ensured he got a run at the Gabba, but the poor times and long odds meant that the Brisbane bookies would treat him as a no-hoper. Unknown to the bookies, though, Prince Regis had, just before the Gabba 700-metre race, smashed the track record over a similar distance in a trial at Orange.

'I put $20,000 on Prince Regis in the 700 metre race at the Gabba and averaged 7/2, meaning I had him going for a $70,000 profit. But almost as soon as the boxes opened another greyhound grabbed Prince Regis by the throat. It fought him for about 500 metres and the two of them were soon hopelessly tailed off behind the rest of the field. When Prince Regis finally shook off the fighter he rocketed after his opponents. But he just failed to catch the leader and finished a close second, so after all that effort I lost my $20,000.'

Ron Nicholas, the now-retired chief steward who put Jack Pringle out, also handed out a second life disqualification. One night at the dogs in the 1980s I asked Nikko if there was any news.

'Oh, I outed a bloke for life this week,' was his reply. The reason for this severest of all punishments was that the miscreant, a little-known hobby trainer, had killed two of his dogs. It seems one Saturday afternoon, the fellow took two greyhounds to Moss Vale track, in the NSW Southern Highlands. He backed them both heavily and each was beaten. On the way home, with rage swelling inside him, the trainer suddenly pulled his station wagon up on an overhead bridge at Pheasants Nest. He calmly got the dogs out of the car and hurled them into the murky water a hundred feet below.

Naturally, horrified motorists took down the registration number of his car and he was apprehended and booted out of the sport. But my colleague Peter Frilingos, the famous *Daily Telegraph* rugby league writer who died suddenly in 2004, loved the retort of the trainer when quizzed by Nicholas. According to the steward, he had said to the trainer: 'Didn't you realise that was a horrendously cruel thing to do to those dogs?' The reply had the chief steward gobsmacked. 'It wasn't cruel. I strangled them before I threw them off the bridge,' came the trainer's response.

This guy was the exception to the rule, as 99.99 per cent of greyhound owners and trainers love their dogs. There's an old saying that a critic can say what he likes about a trainer or his family, but must never denigrate his greyhound. I've learned to be extremely discreet when suggesting that perhaps a greyhound did not chase keenly and was found wanting at the finish of a race. Dozens of trainers have approached me over the years wanting to know my opinion of their dog's performance. In the early days I was totally frank, but have since found that diplomacy is the best bet.

Around 35 years ago a dog chased so poorly during a race that it did everything but pull up. The trainer, obviously looking at his pet pooch's race through rose-coloured glasses, found me later to seek my opinion of the run. When I told him the dog didn't chase, the trainer's eyes bulged, his face turned red, and he screamed: 'You must be fucking blind. He got checked about four times!'

An amazing percentage of NSW's greyhound trainers are Maltese, and most are highly efficient at their chosen hobby. The percentage is extraordinary because there is no greyhound racing on the tiny Mediterranean island. But while the Maltese too love their dogs, the language barrier once caused a heartbreaking situation for Alfred Chircop, who these days trains out of western Sydney.

Freddy, as he is known, got his first greyhound in Victoria in 1963, soon after he migrated to Australia. He was so adept at training that in the first 12 months he won 35 races with giveaways — greyhounds considered so hopeless nobody else wanted them. In 1964 Freddy finally got hold of a smart dog and won a good race with his new star at Warragul on a Friday night. Bright and early next morning Freddy took the dog to his local veterinary surgeon, simply wanting to have the animal checked out for any muscle injuries or soreness. He took 10 minutes in his broken English trying to explain what he wanted from the vet, who nodded in apparent understanding and motioned for Freddy to wait outside. A short time later the veterinary surgeon emerged and handed Freddy his dog's lead and collar — but there was no dog.

It turned out the vet completely misconstrued what Freddy had been trying to convey and euthanised his promising racer. Even now tears well in Freddy's eyes when he tells the story, as he is prone to do for anyone prepared to listen. Apparently when he returned home from the ill-fated veterinary visit, his wife asked: 'Where is de dog?' To which a shattered Freddy replied candidly: 'He killed him!'

Dick Riley, a trainer based in the NSW northern coalfields area near Maitland, is another who will not hear a harsh word said about his dogs. His partner Christine once told me how they headed off to Taree to race one of their team on a Saturday afternoon. Dick placed the greyhound in the boxes while Christine put their money on and watched the race. But each had a different perception of the merit of their dog's performance. After the event, in which the dog ran fourth, Chris ran over to Dick and exclaimed: 'Gee that was a disappointing run, Dick. We'd better not get too rapt up in this bloke.'

However, Dick had thought the dog a certainty beaten, believing it had been bumped several times and had put up a mighty performance. He was so angry with Christine denigrating their pooch's performance that he grabbed the dog, jumped into the car, and headed home. Poor Chris was left to fend for herself, hitching a ride from the racetrack to Taree and having to wait two hours for a bus to get her home. She was philosophical about the incident. 'It taught me one thing; Dick loves his dogs and you must never say anything bad about them to him,' was her summing up.

He almost certainly didn't love his greyhounds any more than anyone else, but retired Cessnock coalminer Bob Hill used to take his bonny stayer Gloavon to the races in style. Hill didn't drive so would hire a taxi to ferry him and Gloavon, the Harold Park 1967 Association Cup final winner, to the state's racetracks. Bob had a bit of a temper and his occasionally fiery personality saw him lose money despite winning a race with his only runner one night at Muswellbrook during the late 1960s.

The taxi fare from Bob's home in Cessnock to Muswellbrook was $14, and first prizemoney for the race was $16. Bob's greyhound won, so he was showing a $2 profit for his night out. But the greyhound's win raised the ire of a section of the crowd. Apparently Bob's dog had performed ungraciously at its previous race, and some of the fans lost no time in letting Bob know this as he proudly led his winner back down the home straight. Fiery Bob repaid his critics in kind, giving the irate punters a return verbal spray for which the stewards fined him $4. Result: a race win and a $2 deficit.

10

My (Brief) Career as an International Tour Guide

These days we seem to have everyone from ex-cricketers leading tours to watch Test series in England to TV gardeners taking people to visit the world's most spectacular flower displays.

But when you hear of so-called celebrity tour leaders getting free trips in return for organising overseas jaunts, don't envy them too much. I became an overseas tour leader on a couple of occasions and believe me, it is not all beer and skittles.

In the early 1970s I was approached by a couple of bookmakers and a few punters suggesting I take a group to greyhound tracks around the United States. I made a few inquiries and my old mate Bob Fulton, who ran a travel agency at the time, offered me what sounded like a good deal. I was to have my accommodation paid in return for organising the group of around 20 people, and would only need to pay my airfare.

But Jack Woodward, the editor of the *Greyhound Recorder*, had led a couple of similar junkets and advised me I could do better from Grace Bros Travel, with whom he had been involved. Charlie Gibson, the former boss of South Sydney Rugby League Club, was in charge of group travel there. He not only offered to look after my accommodation and pay my airfare but also to give me something like $40 spending money for every tour participant over and above 16 people. Bob, like me a dyed-in-the-wool Manly-Warringah supporter, wasn't too happy about me jumping into bed with an ex-Souths man but hey, I had to look after number one.

Thankfully I knew most of the people among our little band of travellers, and they were an easygoing bunch. Otherwise I reckon I'd have had an ulcer after just a few days. Our first port of call was San Francisco, as while there was no dog racing there it was a good entry point and we were going to do the tourist bit as well as taking in the greyhounds. According to the tour blurb each of my team had received from Grace Bros Travel, all porterage was included. That meant it was my job to organise porters to collect the group's bags and take them out to the waiting bus.

No problem there. But one of our group, a guy called Keith who had never previously left his country town in NSW, became a bit agitated. 'There's a porter over there, I'll call him over to organise these bags,' he sang out to me. Before I could stop him, our friend from the bush bellowed out: 'Hey, Sambo! Hey, Sambo!' to the African American porter some 25 metres away. I lunged across the assorted baggage and thrust my hand across Keith's mouth. 'You'll get us killed,' I told him. 'Don't you know that is an extremely derogatory term?' Keith didn't really mean anything by it. He just didn't know any better. He had probably grown up as a kid reading that old children's book about Little Black Sambo and was too naive to realise what an offensive thing he had said. But worse was to come.

When we got out of the airport our bus had failed to arrive. I called Gray Line and the operator drawled, 'We have you down for an 11 am arrival.' My reply was: 'I don't care what time you've got us down for. It's 10 am and we're here.' He said it would take 30 minutes or so to get a bus to us and meanwhile I had to re-confirm our flights to Las Vegas, scheduled for a couple of days later. When I arrived at the United Airlines desk it was boarded up with a sign advising the public that they were on strike indefinitely. What an introduction to my free trip! Finally, with the help of a couple in our group, especially bookmaker Peter McCullen who was a seasoned traveller, we got sorted out and jumped on the bus. Unfortunately we had arrived smack dab in the middle of Chinese New Year and the poor old driver had a horrendous time avoiding street closures and parades by weaving through back alleys to get us to our hotel.

After a marathon trip we lobbed at the Drake Wiltshire Hotel, which was centrally located. I was most impressed by a sign in the foyer which read 'Welcome to Jeff Collerson and Party from Down Under'. But while I was registering the group two interstate bookies in our group approached me. They looked worried and one said: 'Mate, do you realise we are the only white people in this hotel?' I looked around the foyer and while the staff behind the reception desk and the guests sitting in lounge chairs were indeed all African Americans, I couldn't see the problem. The hotel was old and had probably seen better days but appeared to be clean and, most importantly for a short visit, seemed to be right in the middle of the action.

But I no sooner flopped on my bed than there was a knock on the door with the two bookies and their wives telling me they were checking out and moving to the posh St Francis Hotel across the street. I told them I didn't know if they would get a refund on the accommodation part of their trip but they weren't worried about that. They just wanted to know what time we were leaving next morning for our bus tour of Fisherman's Wharf.

Highlight of our greyhound itinerary was to be a visit to the Greyhound Hall of Fame, in Abilene, Kansas. But first we went to Florida, America's home of greyhound racing, where the dogs attract attendances equal to thoroughbred racing and where the tracks are privately owned. I had organised some hospitality in advance and at places like the Hollywood Dog Track, Miami, it was truly breathtaking.

When our fleet of taxis arrived the public relations director of that track was waiting for us with a bundle of souvenirs, race-books, and so forth. During the race meeting one of our group, a dog trainer from Lithgow, remarked that he had so far had no luck buying an American box muzzle to take home with him. Although he would not be permitted to use the American-style muzzle when he raced his dogs, he was keen to create a talking point when he trialled his greyhounds back home. As the dogs completed the first race, I noticed the public relations guy in the catching pen waiting for them. When the first greyhound entered, the PR fellow whipped its muzzle off, raced up to the restaurant where we sitting, and said to the Lithgow trainer: 'There you go. Compliments of Hollywood Dog Track.'

While in Miami a few of us also visited the local jai-alai stadium. Jai-alai (pronounced 'high lie') means 'merry festival' in Basque and is among the world's oldest ball games. If you get a chance to see this spectacular game (the US also has stadiums in Las Vegas and Connecticut) don't pass up the opportunity. Jai-alai is a bit like squash but its promoters claim it requires more skill, stamina and playing nerve than any other sport. The jai-alai racquet, called a *cesta*, is actually a wicker basket. It has a frame made of steam-bent chestnut with form-shaping ribs planed down to 1/16th of an inch thick by one inch wide. Reed, which is imported from Spain's Pyrenees Mountains, is woven over the frame and ribs. The player inserts his hand into a leather glove sewn to the outside of the *cesta* and a long tape is wound around the glove to prevent the hand from slipping out. During play the rock-hard ball, called a *pelota*, must be caught on the full or after no more than one bounce. Competitors must catch and throw the ball in one continuous motion. Massive betting is placed on jai-alai games, which are played, like tennis, as singles or doubles matches.

Being always keen to seek out a top-notch restaurant when in a new city, I asked the PR man at Miami's Hollywood dog track where we should eat when we reached Abilene. He looked incredulous and replied: 'Listen. Abilene is a one-horse cowboy town, don't expect to find any fancy eateries there. My best recommendation would be in the bowling alley. It is called the Strike 'n' Dine.' Abilene turned out to be a lovely, friendly place though, having become famous in America as the place where Dwight 'Ike' Eisenhower was raised. We stayed in the Eisenhower Motor Inn, and in fact every second place seemed to be the Eisenhower something or other. But I got a shock when I went to a bank to cash some traveller's cheques. The teller drawled: 'Gosh, you're from Australia. I've never seen anyone from Australia. What are you doing in Abilene?'

When I told her I had brought a group to visit the Greyhound Hall of Fame she looked at me in disbelief. 'No such place exists here,' she said. 'Maybe it's in Abilene, Texas, which is a much bigger place.' I was mortified. Don't tell me I had brought my group to the wrong Abilene! Thankfully we were right and the bank teller was wrong. The Greyhound Hall of Fame was indeed, and still is, housed in Abilene, Kansas, apparently because the sport had its birth in America in that town. The Hall of Fame was fabulous, and our group got a real buzz out of studying a lavish tribute to Chief Havoc, the first Australian dog to be inducted there.

Jack Millerd from Gunnedah had bought Chief Havoc as a puppy for £16 8s. and used to carry Patches, as he called his dog, around in the back of a utility. Chief Havoc had his first race at Grafton during the 1946 Easter carnival and won. Two days later he ran the fastest 440 yards ever run at Grafton, and by the time he retired in January 1948 had broken or equalled 19 track records. Chief Havoc won 26 of his 36 races but Jack Woodward, the doyen of greyhound writers and long-time editor of the *Greyhound Recorder*, told me once the dog was never beaten on his merits.

Zoom Top, who was the NSW Greyhound of the Year in 1968 and '69, is clearly the best I've seen. Chief Havoc was before my time but those who have seen both these greats, like Woodward and Ambrose Murray, who has been involved with greyhounds since the sport's Australian launch in 1927, agree he was superior to Zoom Top. The highlight of Chief Havoc's illustrious career came in May 1947, when 17,000 people crammed Harold Park, Glebe, to watch his solo attempt on all existing track records.

A series of flashing lights illuminated each race distance point, the idea being that if Chief Havoc reached the point before the light sparkled, he had broken that existing record. Starting from the 800-yard boxes, Chief Havoc broke the 440-, equalled the 500- and then broke the 660-, 700-, 750- and 800-yard records. Races had been, on various occasions, run over these six distances at Harold Park, and the Chief matched or bettered every previous best time. Chief Havoc was as successful at stud as he was on the racetrack, and no doubt a sequence of wins by his offspring which went to America sped up his induction into the Hall of Fame there.

Chief Havoc is buried under a tree at Gunnedah Racecourse, and for years the racebook at the local dogs immortalised his deeds in a poem penned by a greyhound fan called Neville Fisher. It read:

> Now gather round you punters and bookies here tonight,
> We want to draw attention to an important oversight,
> There's a wonder dog in question made coursing history,
> This hound was named Chief Havoc and is buried by
>   this tree,
> And sometimes on a race night, when the bunny starts
>   to whirr,
> And the traps spring loudly open, the old Chief stirs,
> And listens 'til the punters have all gone home, too soon,
> Then he has a final gallop by the pale light of the moon.

After Abilene, our group headed to Mobile, Alabama, where one of America's most famous greyhound tracks can be found. When we arrived I bought a newspaper to check out the fields for that night's racing. There wasn't a line about greyhounds, or any other form of racing for that matter, and once again I was a bit worried whether we had come to the right place. But that night we got a real taste of Southern hospitality, with a huge centrefield semaphore board flashing, rather embarrassingly: 'Welcome to Jeff Collerson and his mates from Down Under!' I quizzed our host from the Mobile club as to why there was no publicity about the races, which, amazingly, drew a crowd of around 20,000.

He explained: 'We are in the middle of the Bible belt here. Horse and harness racing are banned and we consider ourselves fortunate to be allowed to exist. We just let things run along as we don't want to antagonise anyone who might accuse us of trying to entice people to gamble. There is a large orphanage in Mobile and a few years back we wanted to stage a Christmas exhibition race meeting, devoid of any form of betting, purely for the kids. We had arranged for Santa to fly in by helicopter to hand out gifts to each of the orphans. But our legal people advised us against it, saying we would run the risk of being charged with promoting gambling. The legal advice was that the exercise would cost us a lot of money yet would likely garner unfavourable, rather than approving, comment and publicity.'

Travel mishaps always fade with time, and we tend to look back on adversities with amusement rather than stress. That's why a year or so later I was ready to go again, this time taking in Europe as well as America. The highlight was to be a visit to Pat Dalton's stud farm at Golden, in Tipperary. Dalton was, and still is, considered the leading owner/breeder in the world, and has large teams of greyhounds racing in Ireland, England and the United States. I had interviewed Pat a couple of years earlier when he had visited Australia, so was confident we would be well looked after.

Sure enough, when our bus rolled up outside their door, Pat Dalton and his wife were waiting and invited our 20-strong group in for tea and scones. Then it was time to look at his breeding farm and racing kennels. Pat was leading us around, pointing out some of the world's great greyhounds, when one of our group, a trainer from southern NSW, piped up. 'Hey, mate,' he said, addressing the legendary Dalton, 'I hope you don't expect to rear any champions here. This soil is too sandy. If you raise pups here they'll grow up with splayed feet and won't be able to gallop properly.'

I nearly choked. Here was a guy who had trained maybe two winners at Dapto in the past decade, instructing the world's top greyhound man. But Dalton was, as always, most polite. He replied quietly: 'Yes, I've heard that theory about not being able to raise good pups on sandy soil. But I think we have proved it is an old wives' tale. Right where you're standing is where Rocking Ship was born and raised, and he has just won the Irish American International and been ranked the best dog in the United States.'

People slag off Americans as being noisy and brash when they are in a group, but Australians, at their worst, would give them a run for their money. The funniest part of that European trip came when we decided to take in a race meeting at Tralee. On the way to the track our bus driver, Brian O'Brien, entertained us with humorous stories about the locals.

He came up with all the old Irish jokes we hear in Australia, such as 'Did you hear about the Irishman who wanted to go water-skiing so searched the world for a sloping lake?' Only Brian's version had each object of ridicule coming from County Kerry. Although we had told nobody about our visit to Tralee, when our bus pulled up an elderly gentleman ran out to greet us. 'Are you Mr Collerson from Australia?' he inquired. When I told him that indeed I was, he introduced himself as 'Mr Lynch', the secretary of the Tralee Greyhound Club. He then asked how many of us would be attending his club's race meeting. When I informed him that 13 of our 20-strong group were on the bus, he grimaced and muttered: 'Thirteen. Jesus Christ and I'm to let you all in for nothin'.'

Apparently Moneta Holland, whose husband Pat was secretary of Ireland's Greyhound Control Board, had phoned ahead and said that if we arrived we were to be given complimentary admission. I assured Mr Lynch we would prefer to pay the £1 fee, but he would have none of it. Just the same, as the turnstile clicked over 13 times he stood there with his hands in his pockets muttering, 'Thirteen, Jesus Christ, thirteen. Jesus Christ.' No matter. I reckon the bookmakers and the tote at Tralee dogs achieved record turnover that night, as in our group were several of Australia's biggest punters. A couple of scruffy-looking kids soon latched onto Sydney punter Gary Manning and began tipping to him. Gary was a noted big tipper and when these kids landed a winner their faces lit up as he presented them with their highland fling.

Naturally I took our group to the Lido, that famous Paris nightclub which had bewitched me back in 1972. I gave the place a big build-up, and was stunned when the opening act trotted out. Instead of a spectacular underwater ballet or helicopters flying over our heads, it was a dog act! Out came a tall skinny bloke with a fox terrier and a cocker spaniel. En masse, the group looked at me incredulously. Then came a comment along the lines of: 'You're kidding, Pigeon. A hundred bucks for this. You can see this at Rooty Hill RSL any day of the week.' I stammered back that apparently the Lido had lost a leg since I was last there. But I should have known better.

After the foxie did a few typical dog act stunts, like jumping through fiery hoops, the place was plunged into darkness, there was a massive drum roll, and the spotlight focused on the tall skinny bloke. That's when the cocker spaniel, which had not struck a blow until this point, took centre stage.

The spaniel sat impassively as the tall bloke, with drum roll continuing, put his head on top of the dog's head and kicked his legs up into the air with his arms outstretched. For about 10 seconds the cocker spaniel balanced his master atop his tiny head. 'You see, you doubters, I told you this was a good joint,' I shouted to our group, quietly relieved that the Lido had not let me down. Even now, when I tell the story, people doubt me. 'How much had you lot had to drink?' is the general tone of the banter. But I swear the cocker spaniel balancing the man on his head at the Lido is true. And I have about 20 witnesses.

We also ran into some unexpected good fortune during a stopover in Singapore on the way home. We were staying at the Hyatt where another guest happened to be Billy Bumps, a larrikin character from the eastern suburbs I'd met while he was working for bookmaker Brian 'Porky' Wylie at the dogs in Sydney. Bumps, who also was a part-time model among other things, was living like a king. He explained he was the manager of Singapore's leading jockey, Terry Finger, a former Melbourne-based hoop. We had a couple of great evenings out with them, always in company with Finger's bodyguard. Built like a brick outhouse, the Chinese bodyguard's favourite party trick was to split a whole watermelon with a single thrust of his index finger. Terry Finger had apparently once run into a bit of strife with officialdom in Australia but was exonerated when my old boss, Keith 'Punchy' Robbins, came out in print in his defence. When Finger discovered I was a mate of Keith's the hospitality was really laid on in spades.

11

The Mirror Sporting Editor
Stalks Julie Andrews

Until the *Sun*'s closure in March 1988, which left the *Daily Mirror* as Sydney's sole afternoon newspaper, there was fierce rivalry between the Fairfax-controlled *Sun* and the Murdoch-owned *Mirror*. Being the sporting editor or editor of either paper was like being caught in a revolving door. Working in the sporting department of the *Daily Mirror* from 1968 until the paper merged with the *Daily Telegraph*, I reckon I had 20 different bosses. The reason was that if the *Sun* crept ahead in sales, the axe tended to fall on the head of the editor or sporting editor of the *Mirror*. And no doubt the same applied over at the *Sun*'s Broadway offices.

The first edition of the afternoon papers would hit the streets around 11 am and the editors and sports editors of the *Mirror* and *Sun* would be sweating on the rival tabloid hitting their desks — usually around an hour earlier. If the *Sun* carried a sensational back-page story that the *Mirror* had somehow missed, we in the sports department would be sent scurrying to telephone our sources who would confirm, or preferably for us, deny the truth of the rival paper's scoop. An exclusive in the *Mirror* was greeted with great enthusiasm by the editors and usually warranted an old-fashioned pat on the back for the journo involved.

Peter Miller, now retired on the Queensland Sunshine Coast, along with Pat Farrell, John Wallis and John Moore, were among the best sporting editors in my time. But poor old Peter was certainly tested by his staff at times. I'll never forget one Tuesday morning in our Holt Street office when the *Sun* lobbed onto his desk. There was a racing story so big that it was not on the back page, but on the front. The *Sun*'s yarn told the tale of leading jockey Des Lake being involved in a horrendous track fall earlier that morning. Lake had been riding trackwork at Warwick Farm when his horse crashed to the turf. The famous hoop had been rushed to hospital in a critical condition.

The *Daily Mirror* did not have a single line about the mishap. Peter Miller, ashen-faced, called out from his desk for our Warwick Farm trackman. 'Were you at the track this morning?' Peter inquired. 'Sure,' came the reply. 'Well what about this?' asked Peter, pointing to the front page of the old currant bun (the *Sun*). 'Oh yes, I've never seen a worse fall,' said our hard-nosed reporter. 'At first I thought Des Lake had been killed. He didn't move. I reckon he is in a bad way.' Peter Miller looked at him in utter disbelief. 'Didn't it occur to you to phone through a story about a momentous incident like this?' he queried. The answer he received knocked Peter for a loop.

'Listen, boss,' said the trackman. 'I had a stopwatch in one hand, another in my other hand, and a pair of binoculars around my neck. If I'd stopped to phone through a story I would have missed a dozen track gallops!'

Obviously our man did not quite have his priorities right, although he was a punter, so in hindsight he probably reckoned clocking the trials was more important to him than detailing the smash-up of one of Sydney's leading jockeys.

Another incident which caused poor old Peter Miller plenty of angst came in 1971 when the naming of the NSW Harness Racing Horse of the Year was imminent. The *Daily Mirror*'s harness racing writer, Harry Pearce, had been on the voting panel, and although the ballot was secret he was certain a horse called Rocket Glenfern had won. The *Mirror* thought this was a great chance to get the jump on the *Sun* so organised a photographer, along with Harry, to visit the Mona Vale stables of the horse's trainer, Joe Ilsley.

The angle of Harry's story was that Joe had trained Rocket Glenfern by swimming him in nearby Bayview. As well, the unconventional Ilsley always dressed Rocket Glenfern in two sets of trousers, held up by braces, to keep the flies off the horse's precious legs. The *Mirror* secured a stack of great photos of Rocket Glenfern in his pants and more of him enjoying a swim. The back page was made up and the paper on the verge of going to press when the official result was announced. The winner? Bay Foyle!

Harry almost had apoplexy and rushed to a pay phone (no mobiles then) to call Peter Miller. 'Scrap the back page, Peter. Rocket Glenfern didn't win!' Peter retorted: 'You imbecile, Harry, what have you done to us?' It seems Harry had misread the mood of the voting panel, and later blamed his mate, the *Sydney Morning Herald*'s harness racing writer Bill Whittaker, for misleading him as to how he had voted. The last-minute dumping of the back page created havoc in the office, with another story having to replace the trot yarn. And the inside page which was left vacant accordingly had to be filled for the first edition with what's called in the business a 'house ad'. That's an advertisement for one of the paper's own company magazines or newspapers, which in those days were held in the printing room in case of an emergency. And this sure fitted the bill.

Despite those mishaps I'm sure Peter Miller enjoyed his time at the *Mirror*, as there was always plenty of repartee and levity mixed in with the hard work, and we tended to socialise together with our wives and girlfriends. He still loves telling the story of when the office copy boy, who is now the editor of a major daily newspaper, was sent out to buy the lunches. Mike Hurst, now the chief athletics writer on the *Daily Telegraph*, requested 'a peanut butter sandwich with no butter'. The copy boy, obviously bewildered by the order, arrived back in the office with two slices of bread and a bag of peanuts!

Pat Farrell loved the punt, Jack Daniel's and Julie Andrews, not necessarily in that order. His obsession with the star of *The Sound of Music* would these days probably be construed as some form of stalking. He had seen the movie a dozen times, could quote the script verbatim, and when he had a few drinks would usually attempt to phone Julie Andrews, with whom he was absolutely besotted.

Not surprisingly he had little luck, but one day Pat arrived at work absolutely glowing. No doubt using his 'overseas journalist' patter, he had not only tracked Julie Andrews down but had managed to have a three-minute chat with her. It was amazing. Here was this tough, hard-nosed newspaper man of the old school who was absolutely turned to jelly by a Hollywood movie star. I don't think Pat ever phoned her again. That chat with the famous actress satisfied him for life.

Like many of his ilk, Pat Farrell was a very lonely guy. He lived alone in a small flat in Kings Cross but none of us knew much about his family background. One Christmas Doug Phillips, who was the vice-president of the National Coursing Association, one of the two city greyhound clubs, asked Pat what he was doing come December 25. 'The same as I do every year. I'll be sitting at home by myself drinking whisky. I hate fucking Christmas because all my mates are involved with their families. I can't wait for it to end.' Doug, who lived at Schofields, out near Windsor, was astounded. 'Well, you won't be doing that again. I'll pick you up Christmas morning and you'll be joining me and my family for lunch.'

On the big day knockabout Pat was reduced to a flood of appreciative tears when a couple of Doug's grandchildren presented him with presents from under the Christmas tree.

Doug Phillips was probably the best official that greyhound racing in Sydney ever had. He had a great rapport with the sporting editors of the *Mirror* and the *Sun* and was also a great mate of the top journos such as Bill Mordey and Ernie Christensen. He made it his business, at least once a week, to join us journos at our local watering hole, which in those days was the Invicta Hotel, in Elizabeth Street, Surry Hills. The Invicta was owned by the famous ex-pug Vic Patrick and we had some great times there. When it was sold we moved on to the Clock Hotel, in Crown Street, and later to the Evening Star, just down the street from the News Limited office.

Not only did the affable Doug's constant social contacts with Sydney's sporting editors and journalists help greyhound racing get stacks of publicity, but he also worked non-stop to promote the sport through staging special events at Wentworth Park. At one stage he organised for the great athlete Ron Clarke to make an attempt on the world two mile record between races at Wenty and on another occasion arranged for Australia's women sprinters from the 1960 Rome Olympics to stage an exhibition race during the Wentworth Park greyhounds.

In 1964 Doug arranged for the African American Bobby Hayes, who had broken the world's 100 metres record at the Tokyo Olympics that year, to make his sole Sydney appearance at Wentworth Park. Doug organised a press conference for when Hayes stepped off the plane at Mascot. But when Doug dashed out to greet him, Hayes snapped: 'Fuck the press conference. Find me a doctor quick. I've got the clap.' Fortunately for Doug, he persuaded Hayes to talk to the press briefly before chauffeuring the world's fastest man to his family doctor. Much to Doug's relief, the doctor did manage to get the flying machine to Wenty for his exhibition run.

In June 1972, Doug Phillips also launched the annual Celebrity Hurdle, which featured sundry journalists, radio and television personalities racing, under handicap conditions, a full lap of Wentworth Park over brush hurdles. Despite my defeat years earlier by a one-legged Mike Agostini, I contested this event a couple of times, and after being trained in 1972 by Mike Hurst, the *Mirror*'s athletics writer, I almost won. I was one of the front markers that year and held a huge lead at the top of the straight. But my legs turned to jelly as the final hurdle loomed up and I tired so badly I finished fourth. I actually toppled over at the finish line, bringing the radio/TV star Ron Casey down with me.

12

World's Cleverest Dogs
Betting Coup

The biggest plunge ever landed at the dogs was in the UK back in 1979, where the perpetrators fleeced the betting shops for £300,000. Now in those days, a British pound was the equivalent of $2 Australian, but of course the real bonanza reaped by the scam-artists would equate to a heck of a lot more money, in today's terms, than $600,000. The massive fleecing of many of England's 15,000 betting shops didn't even take place at one of the UK's major tracks like Walthamstow, Wembley or White City. The brilliantly executed coup was at a tiny, slightly impoverished track called Rochester, in Kent.

The genesis of the plunge began in Ireland, but by the end of the afternoon's racing that Saturday in July, England's bookies weren't cracking any jokes. Jack Purvis, a trainer from Leysdown, Kent, had purchased two high-quality Irish sprinters, named Band Major and Rathaskar Stuart. Upon their arrival in England, the dogs' names were changed, as was the normal procedure, to Leysdown Fun and Leysdown Pleasure. England's racing rules decreed that for their first few starts in their new home, the dogs' former names had to appear in formguides and racebooks alongside their new titles. So for these few races Purvis entered his pair of short-distance dogs for long-distance events. Naturally, they failed miserably, and their recent form, which was soon all that appeared in racebooks, became laughably poor.

Meanwhile a South London bus operator named John Pocknell offered to sponsor a race series at the Rochester track. Pocknell agreed to put up £200 prizemoney on the proviso that the novelty event be called the Long and Short Trip Stakes. He explained to Rochester officials that his bus company was both a long and short haul operator, so, to get maximum publicity for his firm, he wanted the race's heats staged over 277 metres, with the final a marathon 900 metres. Because of these somewhat bizarre conditions, Rochester secretary Kevin Barry was initially reluctant. But his struggling club could ill afford to refuse a £200 sponsorship. And he could see some curiosity value in the event.

Leysdown Fun and Leysdown Pleasure were duly drawn in the two short-course heats, but by this time their good Irish sprint form, along with their former names, had been expunged from the guides. Punters assumed trainer Purvis was hoping to qualify for the marathon final, which, according to the dogs' form, seemed their only possible chance. But Purvis had no intention of even contesting the final. He and his mates were planning a nationwide betting plunge in the sprint heats.

His first starter, Leysdown Pleasure, was unwanted in the betting, with Purvis ensuring none of his colleagues placed any money on at the Rochester track. Relishing being back racing in a sprint, Leysdown Pleasure blitzed his rivals, a group of plodding stayers entered to try and have a crack at the long-distance final. Leysdown Pleasure started at 33/1. The ease of the dog's win caused a few punters at the Rochester track to guess that Leysdown Fun might have a chance too. His price tumbled down from double-figure odds to 4/1 but it didn't concern Purvis greatly, as that dog also won as he liked. And why would Purvis be worried? His dogs had just landed the biggest betting plunge in the history of greyhound racing.

A band of punters associated with Purvis and the bus company boss had spent the entire day quietly moving around England's betting shops placings bets on the two dogs. To avoid arousing suspicion, they did not place any big bets, limited their wagers to £5 and £10 units, and making £1, £2 and £3 'all-up' bets on Leysdown Pleasure and Leysdown Fun. Because the betting shops — there is no TAB in the UK — offered fixed-price odds rather than a totalisator where dividends are governed by the amount of money placed on a horse or dog, the punters cleaned up. And with the bookies preoccupied with the important thoroughbred meetings being held on a busy Saturday afternoon, they paid no heed to the dribble of £5 and £10 wagers being made on an obscure provincial dog meeting.

That all changed when the shops tallied up their day's transactions and, after contacting bookmakers in nearby towns and cities, realised they had been the subject of a clever betting sting. They were mortified when they realised their all-up payout totalled £300,000. They called in the police, and refused to pay the bets. But after an extensive investigation the public prosecutor declared no laws had been broken, and there would be no action taken. Fred Underhill, the chief executive of the National Greyhound Racing Club, examined the circumstances of the plunge and he too announced no rules had been broken. The bookmakers were then ordered to pay up.

It could hardly be called a scam, but in the 1960s at the now-defunct North Melbourne track a bookmaker called Laurie Place was fielding as a win-only operator. In those days it was the responsibility of the bookies to make up their nameplates for their betting boards, and clever Laurie had his surname emblazoned in huge letters, with his Christian name initial in a tiny format.

Stan Cleverley, a leading trainer of that era and a huge punter, walked into the betting ring to check out the price of one of his runners. Quick as a flash, Laurie, noting that his win-only colleagues were offering 5/1 and the place-only bookies even money, put up 5/2. Cleverley was a smart operator but he fell for the ruse. He asked Laurie for $1000 to $400 about his dog.

Laurie wrote out the bet before challenging the trainer with: 'Do you want the same bet again?' Cleverley was taken aback at this dashing betting and was only too pleased to put another $400 on his dog at what he thought was a luxurious place price of 5/2. When the dog ran third, Cleverley patted himself on the back for bypassing a straight-out wager and strolled over to Laurie's stand to collect his $2000. 'Those tickets are worthless, the dog ran third,' said Laurie as he tore up the briefs. Cleverley replied: 'But you're a place bookie. It says so on your board.' A gleeful Laurie retorted: 'That's my name, mate, that's my name. I'm a straight-out bookmaker.'

While Laurie Place's ploy was relatively innocuous, there have been some insidious attempts to rig races. Fortunately, thanks to alert action by the stewards, few have come to fruition. Although the first race at Sydney meetings is not held until 7.30 pm, stewards are in attendance more than four hours earlier. Their pre-race duties include checking the racing kennels, the starting boxes, the track surface and the mechanical lure mechanism. At kennelling, a little over an hour before the first race, each dog is weighed. A discrepancy of one kilogram from its previous racing weight results in an automatic scratching.

Ron Nicholas, now retired, one of NSW's most capable stewards, reckoned the most sophisticated device he encountered came in 1979. At the time of the incident he told me: 'We discovered jets filled with ammonia which had been dug into the turf in front of the starting boxes. The culprits had plungers spaced from 50 to 100 metres from the boxes which could have been used to spray ammonia into the face of any particular dog. We even found a couple of these plungers in the adjacent car park, which had also been connected to the jets.

'Another scam attempt was when we found someone had drilled holes in all but the number one and eight starting boxes. The holes contained water jets which led to a hose, secreted underneath the starting boxes. The hose had been connected to a tap outside the track. On another occasion we obviously disturbed someone because we found two screwdrivers on top of the starting boxes. Closer examination showed three of the eight boxes had been wired up by transformers. Boxes one, four and eight had live wires running down the inside which could have been set off by a remote-control device.'

Not all cases of on-track interference have been the work of race-riggers. Some were simple vandalism. On 16 April 1979, a gum-like substance was used in an apparent attempt to sabotage a Wentworth Park race meeting. It had been smeared onto the path outside the kennel block and became attached to the paws of 40 of the 73 dogs drawn to race that night. Kennelling time had to be delayed while spirits were used to clean the pooches' feet. Around the same time at Gosford stewards found 15-centimetre long spikes embedded in the turf in front of the boxes. If keen-eyed stewards had not found them, every dog racing in the first event would have been crippled.

Other attempts at wrecking meetings included stringing copper wire across the track at Harold Park, a few centimetres above ground level, and placing strands of fishing line between the inside running rail and the outside fence. In the late 1970s there were five separate attempts to undermine Sydney race meetings.

13

It's Moments Like These...

Back in the 1960s the manufacturers of Minties sweets ran a series of cartoon advertisements depicting characters caught in awkward situations with the catchline: 'It's moments like these you need Minties'. I'm sure we've all had our Minties moments, and the two which stick in my mind came in the early 1980s.

By 1980 Catherine and I had a three-year-old son, Nicolas, the spelling being a nod to her French background. We eventually had four kids, the girls, also with French names, being Sophie (born 1984) and Nathalie (1987) and another son, Dion, born in 1980 and the only one I named. I had my say there, calling him after my favourite rock 'n' roll singer of my youth, Dion DiMucci, who as lead singer of Dion and The Belmonts had massive hits with 'Teenager In Love', 'Runaround Sue' and 'The Wanderer'.

Anyhow, by 1980 Catherine and I also owned a golden retriever dog called Raedler. His unusual name came about because a mate of mine, John Raedler, who had worked for Rupert Murdoch here and overseas and more recently has been with CNN, at one stage had a relentless girlfriend. When I say relentless, she was madly in love with John but the affections weren't fully reciprocated. To get some time away from her, John would often concoct a story that he was tied up with work or busy with friends or family. But it wouldn't matter where he was, this tenacious girl would always track him down. Tony Megahey, the sports radio commentator, once quipped to John: 'If they dropped you into the middle of the Sahara Desert she'd find you. She is a dead-set retriever.' Accordingly, Megahey nicknamed John's girlfriend the Retriever. So, perhaps perversely, when we bought a golden retriever puppy we called him Raedler. If we had bought a bitch puppy we had intended naming her after the girlfriend.

Whenever we went on holidays, we would take the dog to Mossville Stud, a famous greyhound farm at Kellyville, not far from Windsor. The owners, Cath and Bill Fletcher, were not only great friends but also highly successful trainers and breeders. They had a spacious property complete with a dam and long enclosed runs. Raedler used to thrive in this canine holiday camp, tearing up and down his own private paddock, trying to keep pace with the greyhound puppies in the adjoining runs, and enjoying daily swims in the Fletchers' dam.

In 1980 we returned from a holiday and headed off to Kellyville to collect our dog. It was to be a quick pick-up, as we had a function to attend and I was already in my suit and tie. The only greyhound who roamed at will around the Fletchers' property was Dawn Moss, a brood bitch who was also their family pet. Dawn Moss had been a marvellous producer, her puppies having included Trella Light, who had smashed the great Zoom Top's race record when she won the NSW St Leger in December 1973.

As I opened the gate of his yard to put the lead and collar on Raedler, he charged past me and attacked Dawn Moss. Why he did it I don't know, as it is rare for any male dog to attack a female. But attack her he did, ripping a great slab of skin from her side. I dived in between them to try and get him away but he was going absolutely berserk. It wasn't until Bill Fletcher, who had been feeding some greyhounds 50 metres away, arrived and gave Raedler a decent kick that the dog let go. The distressed bitch, who was a real mess, took off into the surrounding bush. By this time I too was covered in blood, and when we finally found Dawn Moss I carried her into my station wagon and rushed her to the nearest veterinary surgeon.

I left her with the vet, who advised she would need extensive surgery. A day later I phoned to inquire about Dawn Moss' progress and Cath Fletcher answered the phone, assuring me she was fine. I called again the next day and got the same response, but Bill answered my following call and admitted their prize brood bitch had gone into shock on the operating table and died.

You can imagine how I felt. Bill's theory as to our normally docile retriever's savage attack on a female greyhound was that Dawn Moss was standing alongside our little son Nicolas, and perhaps he thought she was a threat to him. Whatever the reason, the Fletchers insisted that I still bring our dog to their place whenever we went away because they were still extremely fond of our pooch. I did, however, go out of my way for the next couple of years to try and write lots of nice things about the Fletchers' stud dogs.

Bill Fletcher was a terrific bloke, a rough diamond who had been brought up in an orphanage, been a highly ranked professional boxer (he once fought Vic Patrick) and married Cath, his childhood sweetheart. He was responsible for one of the funniest incidents ever at a big greyhound race presentation after his dog Acclaim Star won the 1979 National Sprint Championship in Perth.

The then premier of Western Australia, Sir Charles Court, made the presentation to Bill. Clutching his trophy, Bill had to respond. Bill was no after-dinner speaker but he thanked the club for staging the race, the sponsor, his wife for her continuing support and the dog's owner for letting him train it. Almost as an afterthought Bill added, turning back towards Sir Charles: 'And I'd also like to thank, umm, what's your name again, mate?' Quick as a flash, Sir Charles, who was obviously a good sport, called out: 'Charlie Court.' Said Bill into the microphone: 'Yeah, and thanks a lot to Charlie Court.' Bill's deliciously impromptu comment brought the place down and had the fans howling with laughter, though nobody enjoyed the incident more than the premier of WA!

Bill had the happy knack of being able to mix with people from every level of society. Among his clients during his career as a greyhound trainer was Sir Robert Askin, the premier of NSW, whose greyhound Marlom Moss, trained by Bill, made the final of the 1972 National Derby at Wentworth Park. Unfortunately Marlom Moss broke his leg a few days after the Derby and had to be retired.

My other most embarrassing moment — apart from the 'best family group' debacle at the Brookvale Show when I was a little kid — came when I took my wife and sons to France to spend Christmas with Catherine's parents.

The Christmas Eve dinner was to be a major event as it was the first time in many years Robert and Marcelline had been able to get each of their four children together, along with their various extended families. Catherine and her mum spent all day in the kitchen, with my job being to go and buy the bread.

There was a *boulangerie* (bakery) on the ground floor but Cath insisted I trek halfway across Paris to her father's favourite baker to buy a range of different breads. She drew me a map of how to get there, but when I got downstairs it was blowing a gale, cold and raining. At that time in Sydney bread came in packets and was either white or brown. To the Frenchman, on the other hand, bread is like wine and cheese; it's a way of life. But because of the weather I decided to avoid the long walk and buy the bread from the shop on the ground floor. Deceitfully, I filled in an hour by popping into an interesting-looking wine shop down the block where I bought a few bottles for the dinner. Then I called into the ground-floor bakery, showed them Catherine's list, and sure enough, was supplied with the lot.

When I got home Catherine asked me if I found the shop okay. 'No problem, it was easy,' I lied. Everything was fine until Catherine's dad Robert sliced the first piece. As soon as he put it in his mouth, he grimaced, winced, and then said to his daughter: 'Where did you buy this terrible bread?' I knew I'd been sprung. Catherine realised at once I had not gone to her father's favourite place, and when I threw myself on the mercy of the court by explaining it had been cold, raining, windy, etc. kindly Robert said: 'No problem. This bread will do us fine.'

Of course Catherine was not too happy with me and when I took off the next day to buy the bread for Christmas Day lunch, I retrieved Cath's map and found the right place. Incredibly, there was a 25-metre queue of people waiting to get in to buy their bread. And just as it had been until I lobbed on Christmas Eve, the shop downstairs from the family's apartment was devoid of customers.

People often bag the French as being rude and arrogant, but I always advise friends who are heading to Paris to learn a few basic phrases before they leave. The French are the most nationalistic people I know of, but if they can see a visitor endeavouring to speak their language, no matter how much it is being mangled, they invariably switch to English and are happy to assist. And like anywhere else in the world, country people tend to be friendlier than their big-city counterparts.

In that 1982 trip Catherine and I, along with Nicolas and Dion (the girls Sophie and Nathalie had not yet been born), arrived back in Paris after a trip to Burgundy. Exhausted after the train trip, we joined a long taxi queue and finally arrived at the head of the line. As a taxi pulled off the rank about 25 metres down the cobble-stoned road, a couple emerged from the station and hailed him. To my astonishment and anger, the cabbie pulled up and helped the interlopers load their bags into his boot. I blew up at Catherine — because she was French — insisting such rude behaviour would never happen in Sydney (as if!).

'Don't worry, this is our taxi,' Catherine assured us. 'Leave it to me.' She then strode down the road, and just before the taxi took off she opened the boot and hurled the cab thieves' luggage onto the road. Naturally the passengers and driver jumped out of the taxi, but Catherine ignored their beseechments and called me and the kids to join her. As the couple left to join the queue, as they should have done in the first place, they seemed to be arguing. I asked Catherine what the husband was saying to his wife. Catherine replied: 'Oh don't worry, they are from the country, they don't know any better. He was saying the equivalent of "there you go, I told you I didn't want to come to fucking Paris for a holiday. We've been here two minutes and had an argument already."'

During that same visit to France I also headed off to Alsace, to taste some wine. This time we decided to separate the kids, with me taking Nicolas and leaving Catherine and Dion with the in-laws. When we went to book our rail fare I discovered that the chef from a famous Michelin-starred Parisian restaurant, called Jamin, was doing a guest cooking stint in the first-class section of the train for the return journey from the Alsace capital, Strasbourg, to Paris.

I paid the extra $100 to go first-class and little Nicolas and I found ourselves sharing a spacious compartment with an American couple who were returning from Germany to Paris to spend three months at the Ritz, as they did each year. The husband, Fred Mustard Stewart, told me he was a writer. 'What a coincidence,' said I, 'I'm a writer too.' Fred explained he was an author of historical novels and that his wife was a New York literary agent. 'I wrote a book called *Mephisto Waltz*, and they made a bad movie out of that, starring Curt Jurgens,' recalled Fred. 'I also did a book called *Nine Weeks*, and they made another bad movie out of that. It starred Dudley Moore and Mary Tyler Moore.' He then explained that his most recent novel was *Ellis Island*, which told the history of the New York quarantine station which had traditionally been the first port of call for migrants coming to America. 'It's now a mini-series starring Richard Burton; it was the last thing he did before his death,' said Fred, a truly interesting and especially affable character. 'Now tell me, what do you write?' Without batting an eye I replied: 'I do the dog form for the Sydney *Daily Mirror*!'

We became friends nevertheless and when we got back to Paris my wife Catherine and I joined Fred and his wife at some restaurants.

I mentioned earlier that our younger son was named Dion, and in 1984 his rock 'n' rolling namesake came to Australia. By this stage he had become a gospel singer, having been through a bout of drug addiction, hitting the skids, and then finding God. His only Sydney concert was to be at the Christian City Church, which was in a huge hall at Dee Why, on Sydney's northern beaches. I told the *Daily Mirror* news editor, Gordon McGregor, there was a good feature article in this born-again former rock star, and volunteered to meet Dion at the airport and get my story. My real reason, however, was to get Dion to autograph a photo of my son, the Australian Dion.

The singer Dion's teenage idol days were long gone of course, and the only people waiting for him at the airport were a representative of his gospel recording company, myself, and Glenn A. Baker, the rock historian. Unfortunately Dion's plane was late arriving, and he was hurriedly bustled past us with his entourage.

'Sorry, fellas, no time for interviews, we have to get to this church to start rehearsing for tonight's concert,' said someone who was apparently Dion's manager. Just as I was thinking what a bummer, Glenn A. Baker called out: 'Gee, Dion, that's a pity. This guy named his kid after you!'

That did the trick. Dion, by this time 25 metres away, stopped in his tracks, spun around, and pointed to me saying: 'You named your kid after me?' He turned to his manager and band: 'Twenty minutes ain't gonna hurt. I gotta talk to these guys.' I got my interview and had my photo autographed 'To Dion, best wishes from your brother Dion. Always remember, God loves you.'

That night Catherine and I had seats in the front row at Dion's gospel concert. Halfway through, he declared that although he no longer sang pop he would agree to a request to sing just one of his hits. 'I'll sing my first million-seller, "Teenager In Love",' he announced. 'Only trouble is I got no Belmonts now so I need three people to jump up on stage and sing back-up.'

Remembering me from the airport that afternoon, he looked at me and beckoned for me to be an honorary Belmont. To my everlasting regret, I got cold feet. At nearly 40 I seemed to be at least double the age of nearly everyone else in the place and thought the rest of the audience would snigger at this old bloke making a fool of himself. While not singing back-up to my boyhood idol remains the greatest regret of my life, it remains a never-ending source of teasing from the rest of the family.

When it came time for my sons to attend high school, my greyhound contacts came in handy. Catherine, being a Roman Catholic, was keen for them to go to a Catholic private school. I'm a Protestant but have never been a regular churchgoer, so agreed to Catherine's request. The only trouble was that Catholic private schools like St Joseph's and St Ignatius were out of my league financially.

Catherine then heard about St Patrick's, a Christian Brothers college at Strathfield, that was far more affordable. Only problem was that because I was a Protestant, our sons were put near the bottom of the waiting list. A few months before Nicolas' high schooling was to commence, we got a letter saying he would not be enrolled. I then remembered that Jim Carr, the chief steward at Harold Park dogs, a good mate of mine and a staunch Catholic, was a great pal of Father Kevin Manning, who held the position of monsignor in a diocese in the NSW western districts. Father Manning — he is now the Bishop of Parramatta — owned a greyhound called Tivoli Chief, who had been trained by Jim Carr's son, Jim junior, and was the top sprinter of 1970.

Jim senior contacted Father Manning, who kindly wrote to St Pat's, informing the Christian Brothers there what a wonderful family the Collersons were and what an asset our son would be to their college. Nicolas was accepted immediately, and once he was in, Dion had an easy entree three years later. It's the old story. It's not what you know, but who you know.

14

The Mouth of the Hunter
and the Baron of the Barossa

Australian wine has certainly come a long way in the past 20 years, with our exports in 2004 worth more than $2.7 billion. Certainly our vino must be a heck of a lot better than it was back in 1933 when George Orwell made a snide reference to Aussie wine in his book *Down and Out in Paris and London*. Wrote Orwell: 'Comparing convent tea with coffee house tea was as different as a fine Bordeaux to that muck known as colonial claret'.

In February 1988, nearly 20 years after I joined the *Daily Mirror* as its greyhound writer, I added a weekly wine column and wine-related feature stories to my racing duties. People are often incredulous that somebody who writes on greyhounds also dabbles in wine, but why not? English cricket writer John Arlott was also a wine columnist and, after all, people from many different walks of life enjoy wine.

The *Mirror* wine column had been launched by Reg Parkhouse, who was a sub-editor in the sporting department. On Reg's death his son Alan took over the wine column, but when he left for an indefinite overseas break the paper began looking for a new columnist. I threw my hat in the ring, telling then *Daily Mirror* editor Roy 'Rocky' Miller (now editor of the *Gold Coast Bulletin*) I would take a different approach to the column.

I suggested *Daily Mirror* readers were less interested in the technical side of wine and would be more responsive to human-interest articles about winemakers. And I also pledged to introduce a bargain buy review section, recommending wines costing less than $10 which, after all, were what the average punter was most likely to drink.

When Rocky asked: 'How much extra do you think you'll get to do the wine?', I replied: 'I'm not worried about that. I'd just enjoy doing it.' That was the right answer as Rocky retorted, quick as a flash and in his own knockabout way: 'Just as well because you'll get fucking nothing. But it must be worth it in terms of free piss because plenty of other people are keen to do it too.'

For the next fortnight there was no wine column in the *Mirror*, then Rocky called me in and told me I was to be the wine writer on a three-month trial basis.

The first function I attended as a wine writer was hosted by Peter Lehmann, nicknamed the Baron of the Barossa. PL, as he is affectionately known, and his wife Margaret had arranged a luncheon at a posh Centennial Park restaurant to launch their new releases. They had invited wine writers from around Australia including luminaries such as the *Australian*'s James Halliday, the *Sydney Morning Herald*'s Huon Hooke and prolific wine book author John Beeston.

After an hour's tasting it was time to be seated for lunch. Lehmann called out: 'Jeff Collerson, you're sitting up here next to me.' This pronouncement caused quite a deal of consternation, because the seat alongside the host is usually reserved for the guest perceived by the function organisers to be the most important. Yet here was the new kid on the block placed next to PL!

As we sat down, Lehmann said: 'Do you know why you're sitting next to me?' I admitted I was a bit bemused by the honour, to which he replied: 'Well, I own a horse racing in the 3.15 race at Gawler and I forgot to bring my transistor radio. So when Margaret was organising the seating I told her to put you next to me as I figured you'd be the only bloke here with a radio in his pocket.'

I informed Peter that I was not such a complete desperate that I listened to races while I attended wine functions, adding: 'Do you want me to move as I don't have a radio?' Said PL: 'No, you're here now. You can stay.'

Lehmann is an interesting character. The only reason he became a winemaker was to avoid going to boarding school. His father was a Lutheran pastor who died when Peter, born in 1930, was 15. That meant boarding school further down the track for the young Lehmann, so in 1947, just as he was about to be shipped off, he managed to grab a job working at Yalumba in the Barossa Valley.

By 1960 Lehmann had become the winemaker at neighbouring Saltram. During his first year there he made, as a bit of a lark, some wine using apples instead of grapes. Soon after that Colin Preece, a renowned old-time winemaker, visited the Barossa, so Lehmann took a bottle of his apple wine for the great man to try.

Of course the larrikin Lehmann's aim was to trick Preece, who was an Aussie wine icon. After he tasted Lehmann's wine, Preece told the young winemaker: 'I reckon this would have to be the best wine you've ever made, son. It's excellent.' A gleeful Lehmann, figuring he'd caught out this renowned palate, replied: 'But, Mr Preece, that wine is made out of apples!' Unperturbed, Preece shot back: 'Then I suggest you stick to the apples and leave the grapes to us experts.'

Later Lehmann was presented to Queen Elizabeth, who in the 1970s awarded him with the Order of Australia medal for his services to the wine industry. Two nights later Lehmann met the Queen again, this time at a gala dinner. 'They tell me you work in the wine industry,' the Queen told him. Unfazed, the larrikin Lehmann replied: 'Gee, don't tell me you've forgotten me already, Your Majesty. You presented me with a gong a couple of nights ago.'

Lehmann has long been one of the wine industry's most loved characters, one reason for that being the loyalty he showed dozens of struggling grape-growers in 1977. Saltram's owner at that time, Dalgety & Co., suddenly ceased capital spending and informed Lehmann he was not to buy any grapes for the 1978 vintage.

Lehmann was shattered and embarrassed, as he had made a handshake deal with local growers, many of whom were old friends, that he would buy their fruit. So he persuaded his employers to allow him to form an outside company to process the grapes at Saltram for $50 a tonne. Assisted by loans and subscriptions from family and friends, Lehmann was able to buy $2 million worth of grapes, making bulk wine which he then sold to other producers.

That kept the growers going for another year, but when Lehmann was told by his employers he would have to ditch the growers completely in 1979 he quit Saltram in disgust. Instead, more to keep faith with his grower friends than anything else, he formed his own company, Peter Lehmann Wines.

In 1993, after the company which owned Peter Lehmann Wines had been engulfed by a rival and seemed set to be sold to overseas interests, Lehmann again sought investors. This time he raised $9.3 million and bought his company back. He retired in 2002.

There are some fantastic people in the wine world, though they are dying out because most of the real characters are to be found among the older generation. I'm talking about people like the late John Charles Brown and the late Murray Tyrrell.

During the 1990s I used to organise wine dinners at the Manly-Warringah and North Sydney leagues clubs. At a Manly function, we once served the wines of north-east Victoria's Brown Brothers and the host was the family patriarch, John Charles. He abhorred 'winespeak' and hated the elitism that, unfortunately, can still be part of Australia's wine industry.

At the dinner he told the guests: 'When I read columns by wine writers comparing the taste of one of my whites to asparagus, peaches or apricots or a Brown Brothers red to raspberries, blackcurrants or plums I often wonder if I remembered to put any grapes in there!' It was typical of John Charles Brown that when he arranged for family friend Keith Dunstan to write his family's story he insisted it be called simply *Not a Bad Drop*.

Murray Tyrrell was not as gentle a soul as John Charles Brown but they had much in common. Tyrrell was affectionately known as the mouth of the Hunter because he constantly extolled the virtues of his beloved Hunter Valley. And Tyrrell, like Brown, hated the pomposity some wine critics seemed to embrace.

He was second to none as a wine dinner host, because he would invariably blast politicians, wine writers (especially those who preferred and promoted wines he called 'cool climate crap') and anybody else who might have crossed his path lately.

Murray Tyrrell is credited with making Australia's first commercially bottled wine to be labelled chardonnay. That happened in 1971 after he had noticed some grapevines on a neighbouring vineyard, owned by Penfolds, that he believed were chardonnay. At that stage the wine made from these grapes was often blended away with other white grape varieties, and on the rare occasions it was made singly it was branded, incorrectly, as 'white pineau'.

Murray used to delight in repeating the story of how one night he had 'jumped the fence' at Penfolds and 'borrowed' a bundle of these chardonnay vine cuttings. Murray had always believed the variety's correct name was pinot chardonnay because it had been, in its infancy in France, a derivative of two other grapes, one of which was pinot noir. So he labelled his wines 'pinot chardonnay'.

As this grape rocketed in popularity and was being produced by thousands of winemakers, it was only Tyrrell's who persisted in calling theirs pinot chardonnay. Murray's son Bruce begged his father to drop the pinot prefix, believing it only served to confuse consumers. But Murray, typically, stubbornly refused to accede to Bruce's request.

Huon Hooke, the affable *Sydney Morning Herald* wine journalist, occasionally took Murray to task for persisting with the pinot chardonnay tag. So did everyone else, but Huon's criticism, coming from such a highly respected critic and show judge, really upset Murray.

Years later, when he was fighting what ultimately became a losing battle against cancer, Murray felt totally vindicated when results came through from Europe on DNA testing of the chardonnay grape. According to no less an authority than the esteemed English wine writer Jancis Robinson, the grape should really be known as pinot chardonnay.

As sick as he was at the time, Murray was absolutely euphoric with this news. He sent me a detailed fax of the DNA findings, scribbling on the last of its 12 pages: 'It seems this old bloke is not as stupid as everyone seems to think.' A week later I drove to the Hunter to visit him. As I walked into his office at his family's Pokolbin winery, he barked: 'Did you get that fax I sent you, Collo?' When I replied I had brought it with me he yelled: 'Do me a favour will you? Take it back to Sydney, stick it up Huon Hooke's arse and then set fire to it!' That was vintage Murray Tyrrell, and Huon was greatly amused when I told him of Murray's request.

It didn't require DNA testing for Viv Thomson, long-time winemaker and proprietor of Best's Great Western Wines, to discover he had for years incorrectly identified a plot of grapevines. Best's, in Victoria's Grampians region, had been founded in 1866 and the vineyard had always included a healthy crop of a grape variety known locally as 'Miller's Burgundy'.

In the early 1970s a French ampelographer (grape identification expert) visited Best's and congratulated Viv on his pinot meunier crop. 'No, mate, that's Miller's Burgundy,' said Viv. 'I am sorry to argue, but they are definitely pinot meunier and they are magnificent,' replied the Frenchman. Pinot meunier, along with chardonnay and pinot noir, is used for Champagne production, but is rarely vinified as a red table wine anywhere in the world.

Savvy Thomson immediately began to put out bottles of dry red pinot meunier and the wine, for so long mis-branded, quickly gained a cult following.

Another great wine character is Mick Morris, whose ancestors founded Morris Wines in north-east Victoria's Rutherglen in 1859. James Halliday, in his *Australian Wine Companion*, describes

Morris Wines as 'one of the greatest of the fortified winemakers'. Despite that, Mick, who recently handed over the winemaking responsibilities to his son David, remains one of the most modest, self-effacing and laid-back gentlemen you would find.

A few years back I was visiting Rutherglen with my brother Barry and a friend, Gordon Willoughby, who had played two rugby league Test matches for Australia in 1951 but was also a keen wine enthusiast. Chris Killeen, of Stanton & Killeen Wines, had invited us to a winemakers' dinner at Rutherglen's Shamrock restaurant. A requirement of these bi-monthly functions was that all guests brought along an 'interesting' bottle which they wrapped in tinfoil, so during the meal everyone had a stab at guessing the identity of the mystery wines.

Mick was unable to attend this particular dinner, but during an afternoon tasting at Morris Wines he warned us: 'Be careful of what you say.' When I asked why, Mick said: 'Well, most of the local winemakers will be there and some of them bring along something they made themselves. If you get up and say a certain wine tasted like battery acid you might offend someone. Actually I was persona non grata myself at these dinners for a while.'

I couldn't believe that gentle Mick could ever be out of favour with anyone so he went on to explain that at an earlier winemakers' dinner, held during the annual Rutherglen Wine Show, he had brought along a mystery wine which was easily identified as a fortified style and quickly pinpointed as being a liqueur muscat — the style of wine for which Rutherglen has become famous around the world.

But things took a turn for the worse when a couple of leading Rutherglen producers began extolling the virtues of Mick's mystery bottle, with each lavishing praise along the lines of: 'This is undoubtedly muscat from this region. It seems to have an average age of 50 years. It is definitely made from wonderful old material. This wine is why Rutherglen is famous.' When mischievous Mick unwrapped his mystery bottle, it was revealed to be a liqueur muscat all right, but from South Africa!

Things got worse because the Rutherglen Wine Show was being held during that week and a couple of leading Sydney wine writers were also guests at the dinner ... and one of them later reported this embarrassing case of mistaken identity by these hallowed wine experts. According to Mick, he was suspended for three months and all guests were henceforth barred from bringing imported wines.

Despite that brouhaha, winemakers are generally a tight-knit bunch, as evidenced by an incident involving Coonawarra winemaker Doug Balnaves. Balnaves tells the story of when he set off from home to attend an important black tie dinner. Shortly after he left home, he noticed, in the glare of his car's headlights, a Labrador seemingly stranded in a muddy ditch by the side of the road. Another Coonawarra winemaker, Doug Bowen, owned a Labrador called Bollinger, so Balnaves did the neighbourly thing and pulled up.

Clambering out of his car, resplendent in dinner suit, he lifted Bolly, who was covered in mud, out of the ditch and placed him into the back of his car. By this time Doug was himself covered in dirt and gunk, so any chance he had of getting to the dinner in his tuxedo had well and truly gone. But he was concerned that Bolly, who was not very street-wise, was in danger of being hit by a car. As Balnaves wheeled into the driveway of the Bowen property, he was greeted with the loping, tail-wagging apparition of Bolly bouncing up to meet him. 'I still don't know who owned the Labrador I rescued!' laments Balnaves.

Security being what it is now, this couldn't happen these days, but I love the tale Jane Ferrari, now with Yalumba, tells about when she joined Penfolds as a winemaking rookie. 'After I had been there a week I noticed that each day a lot of the cellar workers would arrive with a two-litre bottle of Coca-Cola. But when they left they would still have these big bottles of Coke with them. Naively, I couldn't work out why they brought Coke to work when none of them seemed to drink it. When I finally asked one of my colleagues about this they pointed out that all these bottles came in filled with Coke, but when they left they contained Grandfather Port!' Old stocks of the port were stored in huge barrels around the winery, and with this celebrated Australian fortified wine costing around $80 for a 750 millilitre bottle the workers were doing pretty well at two litres a day.

The upside of being a wine writer is getting to sample lots of great bottles that would normally be out of one's price range. The downside is being dragged around cellars examining the latest winemaking gadgetry. Basically, if you've seen one winery you've seen them all.

For Don Hogg, who at one stage wrote a wine column for Sydney's *Sun-Herald* and *Financial Review*, his pet hate was perusing bottling lines. Hoggy was famous for a run-in he had with the owners of Montana, NZ's biggest winery, when they flew him over for a few days.

Because Montana had paid his fares and were supplying the accommodation, they were understandably keen to make as much use of his time as possible. But the schedule they had set soon had poor old Hoggy exhausted. By the third day he noticed the itinerary allotted a half day to examine a new state-of-the-art bottling line. Hoggy told his hosts he would give that a miss, pointing out he had not had time even to buy a postcard to send home and that there was nothing in a bottling line to interest his readers.

Montana's management insisted that Hogg stick to the itinerary, and a slanging match ensued. Now Hoggy is an irascible sort of bloke and there was no way he was going to be bullied into doing something he didn't want to do, no matter who had paid his airfares, so he gave the bottling line a miss. To his credit, though, he bore no grudge against Montana after their disagreement and on his return wrote a couple of great articles about the company.

Not long after I'd heard the tale of the Montana bottling line blow-up I was with Hoggy at Mitchelton Winery, in Victoria's Goulburn Valley. Mitchelton's winemaker Don Lewis was escorting a group of wine writers around the property, but after a couple of long tastings it was around 2 pm and we were all starving.

'Christ, when are they going to feed us I wonder?' Hoggy whispered to me. I had briefed Don Lewis, a laconic character if ever there was one, about Hoggy's Montana clash. So as we were heading towards Mitchelton's very fine restaurant, Lewis suddenly stopped short and announced: 'Oh, before we eat, I thought we might spend an hour or two checking out our new bottling line.'

All the other journos were in on the joke, so when Hoggy said, quite loudly: 'I can't believe this. Not another fucking bottling line!' it brought the joint down. Realising it had been a well-rehearsed gee-up, Hoggy turned to me and said: 'You bastard, Collerson.'

One of the upsides of wine writing came when I was invited to a posh dinner at Langton's, the Melbourne restaurant, which was being hosted by Italy's Carlo Petrini. He had founded, in 1986, the Slow Food Society, as a protest against the increase of fast-food outlets around the world. Based in a place called Bra, near Alba, in Italy's Piedmont region, Slow Food now has 80,000 members in 50 countries.

Anyhow, a few years back I attended their inaugural dinner in Australia. Guest speaker was legendary wine writer and critic James Halliday. After Halliday's speech, Mr Petrini, who speaks little English, got to his feet and began regaling us in Italian. Of course he had brought along a translator, who would leap up every few sentences and give us the English version of what Mr Petrini had just said.

Then Mr Petrini said something which included a mention of James Halliday. But the place went into peals of laughter when the translator translated Mr Petrini's last comment as: 'And Mr Petrini would like to say how honoured he is to have James Halliday here tonight as he is without doubt one of the greatest myths in the history of wine.'

Apparently, in Italian, myth and legend mean one and the same thing. Of course us Australians' rather warped sense of humour defines 'a myth' as an impostor. So while poor old Mr Petrini was trying to describe James Halliday as a legend, his translator had told us he was a fake! Mr Petrini knew something had gone radically wrong with the translation when his dinner guests were rolling around the floor laughing instead of standing up and applauding.

15

The Crack Winemaker
Who's Allergic to Alcohol

As a journalist I've always been drawn to the human interest side of the world of wine. The people behind the reds and whites we drink tend to be fascinating characters. If their stories were told more often it might counter the elitist aura which unfortunately still surrounds many aspects of the Australian wine world. That elitism holds back consumption through making young drinkers feel intimidated. That's not the case in places like Italy, Spain and France, where wine is treated as it should be, as a beverage which happens to go well with food.

One of my favourite wine tales concerns Bill Calabria, chief winemaker and proprietor of the now highly successful Riverina (NSW) producer Westend Estate Wines. Calabria's finest moment came when a $10 chardonnay he made was judged best-value full-bodied dry white at the 1999 Sydney International Wine Competition, coming in among the top 100 of 1144 entries from 13 countries.

Yet Calabria has never got to drink this or any of the other hundreds of award winners he has made. The reason is he is a teetotaller. 'It's not by choice as I'm no wowser,' says Bill. 'It's just that I'm allergic to alcohol. When I'm putting my wines together at the end of each vintage I just smell them, taste them, and then spit them out. But even without swallowing, at the end of a couple of hours of blending I feel sick and need to rest. Ironically, the next morning I usually look as if I have had a big night on the grog because my eyes are all puffed up and I look a wreck.'

Calabria's sense of smell is incredible. I've been with him in a coffee lounge where his nose has told him whether the milk in his cappuccino has come from a cardboard or a plastic container. No wonder he can spot faults in wine!

Bill's Italian migrant parents Francesco and Elizabeth came to Australia in 1921 and began making wine in their laundry tubs in 1945. At first they had no commercial goals. They simply made wine to enjoy with friends, most of whom were fellow migrants who came from a wine-drinking culture. But by 1979 they had outgrown the laundry pots and pans and were selling 20 to 30 200-litre barrels of bulk wine every week to buyers in Sydney.

That was when Bill took over as winemaker. He says: 'To call what my parents made vinegar-like was being generous. But that's all they and their friends had been used to drinking so they didn't know any better. I became winemaker on the orders of my father. He didn't think it mattered I couldn't handle alcohol. He reckoned I had the right attributes for a winemaker, the capacity to work hard and ability to smell and taste. Then in 1982 I decided that if we were going to compete we should abandon the bulk wine business and endeavour to produce quality wine in bottles.'

These days Calabria's Westend Estate makes 80,000 dozen a year and is among our most successful exporters.

The Miranda family who founded the Miranda brand, another Riverina-born producer, got started in a similar way to Calabria. In 1939 founder Francesco Miranda crushed his first vintage by foot and sent his wine, 'packaged' in 25 litre drums, by train to his customers in Sydney.

Surprisingly, another non-drinking winemaker who is far more famous internationally than Calabria, is California's Randall Grahm, a world wine legend. His Bonny Doon winery, based in Santa Cruz, is among the most famous in the United States.

I discovered Grahm's intolerance of alcohol a few yeas back when we were both visiting Victoria's Mornington Peninsula region. Garry and Margaret Crittenden, who at the time ran the Dromana Estate Winery, had invited us to dinner at their home. I was seated next to Grahm and at the start of the meal was surprised to see him take an ice bucket off the table and place it on the floor between our chairs. The Crittendens, always generous hosts, had the wine flowing non-stop, but Randall did not swallow a drop. During the dinner he had hundreds of sips, but spat every mouthful, somewhat disconcertingly for me, into the ice bucket alongside my leg. His aim would have done William Tell proud. I finished without a single red stain on the leg of my trousers.

As senior winemaker for the giant Beringer Blass group, Chris Hatcher is responsible for the quality of four million dozen bottles each year. There is a supreme irony in that, as Chris' father Gilbert was a Methodist minister who banned alcohol in the family home.

'When I was still a youngster, my sister, who was 10 years my senior, brought home a bottle of Barossa Pearl which she had won in a raffle,' recalls Hatcher. 'Our father wouldn't let her open it and it was dispatched to the basement. I used to go down there and stare in fascination at this evil bottle. There is no doubt that mysterious bottle of wine planted in me the seed of interest in wine. Because years later, when I was midway through a university science degree, I ran out of money for tuition and needed a part-time job. I found one at Adelaide's Wine Research Institute and from there became a research and development officer at the old Kaiser Stuhl winery in South Australia.

'It wasn't until I began working in the wine industry that my mother confessed that her great-grandfather had been Penfolds' first winemaker. When Dr Christopher Penfold died, his wife took over the business and this ancestor of mine was appointed winemaker. He used to be driven around by a young man named Max Schubert, later to find fame as the winemaker who created Penfolds

Grange. Max was a pallbearer at my great-great-grandfather's funeral.'

Dr Penfold had begun making wine in 1845 but at that time his aim was not to sell it as a commercial tipple. A great believer in wine's medicinal value, his goal was to alleviate anaemia, common among his early 19th-century patients.

Jim Barry in 1960 founded the winery bearing his name in South Australia's Clare Valley. Barry had wanted to be a doctor, but was forced to abandon that ambition in 1946 when he failed his Latin examination, in those days a prerequisite to entering the medical course at Adelaide University. Barry went on to become the seventeenth winemaking graduate of the world-famous Roseworthy Agricultural College at Gawler, SA, from where he became winemaker at Clarevale before establishing his own brand.

Among Barry's neighbouring wineries in Clare was Sevenhill. It had been established by a Jesuit order in 1851 with the object of making sacramental wine. Sevenhill, under the guidance of chief winemaker Brother John May, began making wine for the public in 1958.

European influence was behind the introduction to wine of those behind the Hunter Valley's Gartelmann Estate and Western Australia's Evans and Tate labels. Jan Gartelmann spent many years as the private tutor to the children of Silvio Berlusconi, Italy's prime minister.

'Mr Berlusconi owns the AC Milan football club and whenever his team won he would celebrate by opening bottles of vintage Champagne,' says Gartelmann. 'But he also owned a great cellar of reds and whites from around the world and was kind enough to introduce me to many of those brands. He certainly fuelled my interest in wine and then I married a German gentleman named Jorg Gartelmann, who was also a wine enthusiast. When we migrated to Australia we headed for the Hunter Valley and took over a run-down vineyard in the Lovedale area.'

Interestingly, the magpie emblem on the Gartelmann bottles has real significance. 'When we bought the place there was a colony of magpies living on the edge of the vineyard,' says Jorg Gartelmann. 'We were advised to clear it away so we could increase our grape plantings but then we discovered the magpies were killing all the bugs which ate vine leaves and grapes. So the vineyard stayed the same size and the magpie colony remained.'

In 1971 John Tate, a paint manufacturer, toured Europe and became enamoured of the wines he had tasted there. On his return to Australia he persuaded John Evans, his partner in the paint enterprise, to plant vineyards. Tate bought Evans out in 1983, and now Evans and Tate, these days run by John Tate's son Franklin, is among the fastest growing in Australia.

A trip to France was also the catalyst for the entry into the world of wine of David Lance, whose Diamond Valley Winery, in Victoria's Yarra Valley, quickly became among our most esteemed producers of pinot noir. Lance returned from France in 1969 and formed a wine club, volunteering to be the group's winemaker. He knew the basics of winemaking and was able to buy grapes from Mildura. But his initial results were disappointing so he determined to source fruit from a cooler climate. He was drawn to the Yarra Valley, and after making a few small batches of wine for his friends, produced his first commercial vintage in 1980.

The Melbourne Cup of wine awards, the prize most sought after by wine companies, is the Jimmy Watson Trophy. After winning the Jimmy Watson for a record three straight years during the 1970s Wolf Blass estimated its commercial value to the winning wine was at least $1 million. That's remarkable considering the Jimmy Watson Trophy, awarded to the best one-year-old red at each year's Royal Melbourne Wine Show, was the brainchild of a group of drinkers at a wine bar in Lygon Street, Carlton.

Jimmy Watson, who ran the wine bar from 1935 until his death in 1962, was in the habit of buying young reds from the previous vintage to serve in his bar. After a group of his customers embraced the idea of presenting an annual trophy to the best of these wines, a barmaid named Elsie Gruneklee was enlisted to get donations from regulars to buy the first trophy. In return, they were given a signed picture of Jimmy Watson!

The newest wine area in NSW is the Southern Highlands, centred around the townships of Berry, Moss Vale and Sutton Forest. Although Kim Mogine planted the region's first vineyard, Joadja, in 1983, it was the arrival of a remarkable character some years later that focused attention on the district and led to other vignerons planting grapes. When Leslie Fritz established his Eling Forest vineyard and winery at Sutton Forest in 1990 he was 79 years old. That's remarkable in itself but his tale is even more extraordinary.

When I interviewed him in 1999 he told me he was born in Transylvania, which was renamed Romania in 1918. 'By 1937 I was the manager of a winery and vineyard there,' he told me. 'When World War II broke out, the Jewish owners of the winery were forced to hand over the entire operation to Romanians. Although I was also Jewish I was allowed to stay on because the new owners had nobody else trained to make wine. Our wine production was nearly two million litres a year, while we also made a liqueur made from various herbs and a fortified wine similar to Cognac and brandy. I quit and established my own winery in 1945 but three years later the communists took control of Romania. They insisted I sell the grapes from my nine-hectare property to the communist cooperative for a nominal fee, paying me instead with 200 litres of wine each year. This was the final straw as my father-in-law and mother-in-law had each committed suicide after the communists confiscated their land.

'So I decided to join my cousin, a cosmetic chemist who had emigrated to Australia in 1938. He was living at Randwick and told me that for $1000 he could organise for me and my family to join him. To leave Romania we had to bribe the local authorities with the equivalent of 12 months wages and were not permitted to take any money with us. All we could take, apart from our clothing, was 10 kilograms of salami and five litres of slivovitz.'

But before his departure crafty Leslie Fritz arranged for a dentist friend to secrete a four-carat diamond under a bridge in one of his teeth. During a six-week delay in Austria, awaiting the Australian landing permit to arrive, he was able to sell the diamond for $1052. 'When we got that money, I bought a watch for my late wife Catherine, a transistor radio for my children Peter and Anne and a ticket to *La Traviata* at Vienna's Opera House for myself.' When he finally arrived in Australia in 1962 he worked as an accountant, but moved back into the wine industry after his son Peter bought a holiday home in the Southern Highlands.

16

Greyhound Racing's Quirkiest Tales

Some of the stories I've stumbled upon and the incidents I've encountered over the past 40-odd years are almost in the Ripley's Believe It or Not league. Jack Woodward, the doyen of greyhound racing writers who for several decades edited the Sydney *Greyhound Recorder*, once told me that nobody had ever tipped the program at the dogs. No one has put every winner on a 10-race card on top of his or her selections.

I've tipped eight dozens of times and managed nine out of 10 on three occasions, but the one for Ripley came in the early 1970s at Harold Park dogs. John Nicholls, later to become a thoroughbred horse trainer of note — his father Syd Nicholls had also been a successful Randwick racehorse trainer — was at the time working as a cadet journalist on the *Sydney Morning Herald*.

John was a horse man through and through and was the first to admit he knew little about greyhounds. But during one particular month, because the *Herald*'s greyhound writer was on holidays, John was put in charge of looking after the dog meetings, including doing the tips. He went within an ace of making history one night at Harold Park when he selected the first nine winners. But he missed out on race 10, won by a Victorian-trained dog carrying the moniker of, would you believe it, John Nic.

I've done stories on a seeing-eye greyhound, a vegetarian racer, an escape artist, and others who turned out to be exceptional bargains. In 1978 the champion greyhound in Moree, northern NSW, was Joanne Miller, who won 12 races on her home track. But because she also doubled as a guide dog for her almost blind trainer Vic Hughes, who was unable to travel long distances, Joanne Miller never got to race in Sydney.

Just as Joanne Miller was a godsend for her blind trainer, greyhounds were used as therapy for Vic McGee, who, as a 53-year-old, lost both legs in a 1959 mining accident. McGee, fitted with prosthetic legs, took up greyhound training. Amazingly he had a succession of top-notchers, the star being the rather optimistically named Better Future. She won the 1982 Harold Park Winter Stake final, the Singleton Classic final, the Gosford Goldmine final, the TAB Tracks Championship at Wentworth Park and the Maitland Future Stars final. Not bad for a greyhound trained by a 76-year-old amputee.

In 1988 a South Australian greyhound trainer named Howard Gray won 14 races in succession with a greyhound called Time Machine. A winning streak like that is astounding enough, but Time Machine did not eat meat and raced on a diet of bananas, baked beans and spaghetti!

Sid Swain, who trained Cyrus the Virus, winner of the 2003 NSW Golden Easter Egg, then Australia's richest race, once had a bitch who was impossible to restrain. The aptly titled Proper Houdini was so anxious to escape the confines of her kennel she would, according to Sid, 'pull three-inch nails out of the wire with her teeth'. Sid's wife Lorraine then came up with the notion that maybe Proper Houdini hated her kennel because she wanted to be out in the sun. After Lorraine began spending a couple of hours daily sitting out in their sunny suburban backyard with Proper Houdini, the greyhound, who eventually became a highly successful racer, was happy to return to her kennel each afternoon.

Male greyhounds weigh, on average, about 31 kilograms with bitches around 27. But Linen's Charm, who won a maiden final at Harold Park in January 1970, dwarfed them all. Built more like a Shetland pony than a dog, Linen's Charm tipped the scales at 40 kilograms. Perhaps one reason this giant of the canine world was so big was because he was owned by a butcher, Jim Livingstone, from the western Sydney suburb of Toongabbie. When Linen's Charm won at Harold Park, Livingstone told me that when he had first put the dog into training the animal had weighed 46 kilograms!

The biggest litter I ever wrote about was whelped in December 1970 by a bitch called Cingay, who produced 17 puppies to the leading stud dog, Takiri. And the youngest mum was Roman Senate, who whelped a litter just before her own first birthday. In the 1970s Roman Senate's inexperienced owner decided to take up training the greyhound herself. When her bitch came in season, the naive owner asked an experienced trainer what she should do. Because she neglected to state the age of her greyhound, the old hand told her to get her bitch mated to a 'decent' stud dog. So Roman Senate became greyhound racing's youngest mother.

Prize for the slowest greyhound goes to Babe Cigam, who was owned and trained by Nellie Jones, a nurse's aide who lived in Wigram Street, Glebe, a few metres from the Harold Park trotting and greyhound track. By 1980 the best Babe Cigam had managed in 60 starts was a third in a field of five, but that wasn't even in a race. It was in a trial. At the time Harold Park officials were receiving so many entries for their weekly qualifying trials that they introduced a rule restricting these events to greyhounds which had been placed within their past three starts. So Babe Cigam, too slow to make it into a proper race field, now could not even contest trials. This drove Nellie to distraction because, as she said when I interviewed her for a *Daily Mirror* story: 'Babe Cigam would hear the lure start up at Harold Park and begin running up and down the hallway of my flat.' Nellie eventually overcame this problem by walking Babe Cigam at least five kilometres each afternoon and on race night taking him down to Harold Park to watch the other, faster greyhounds in action.

It is rare, but not unique, for greyhounds to live in a flat. Most successful of this confined group would have to be a dog called Cell Block, who on 1 November 1974 won the Vic Peters Classic at Harold Park, the equivalent of horse racing's Golden Slipper. Cell Block had been raised in the bathroom of his owner-trainer Bill Kotsovolos' flat in Matraville, an eastern Sydney suburb. Because Bill had no backyard, Cell Block spent most of his days watching television in his owner's loungeroom and sleeping in the bathroom. On weekends Kotsovolos, a process operator for a pharmaceutical company, would take Cell Block for walks and gallops along a nearby beach. Cell Block, who was a 33/1 outsider when he won the Harold Park classic, was named after the slang name for the area in which Kotsovolos and his co-workers toiled.

Another TV-watching greyhound was Miss Razzawill, rated Sydney's most promising stayer in 1981. Her experienced trainer Mal Norman was faced with a dilemma when Miss Razzawill, early in her career, was too timid to even take to a racetrack. 'She was terrified of the slightest noise,' Norman told me. 'So I started bringing her into the loungeroom to watch TV. I used to turn the volume up loud and the noise of the television finally settled her down.' Miss Razzawill rewarded Norman's ingenuity by winning the rich Hills Ford Trophy at Wentworth Park in July 1981, landing some big bets at the lucrative odds of 16/1.

The ancient Chinese art of acupuncture saved the career of Queen's Peril, winner of the 1978 Wyong Oaks. She broke a bone in her wrist and the injury became infected. After further complications set in, owner Ron Court was advised to have her foot amputated to avoid the onset of gangrene. But trainer Ken Lee persuaded Court to try acupuncture, a procedure then fairly uncommon in Australia, even for humans. The treatment worked and Queen's Peril returned to a successful racing career.

Stories of bargain buys are legion but my favourites concern a couple of dogs called Tamba's Choice and Ebony Aztec. In the mid-1960s a young man named Robert Green whose father, Digger, was a greyhound trainer, was working at the King Edward dogs' home in Sydney's Moore Park. Among the inhabitants waiting to find a home or be euthanised was an old brindle greyhound named Tamba's Choice. Robert Green bought the dog for the nominal cost of $1 and took him away. Tamba's Choice rewarded his new owner's kindness by winning 20 races for him.

In 1978 Elfriede Tracy went to a greyhound trainer's clearance sale hoping to buy a cheap ride-on lawnmower. Before the mower came up for sale, a scruffy old female greyhound named Ebony Aztec was led into the auction ring. She was unwanted so Elfriede, feeling sorry for the bitch, who was being ridiculed by the crowd, bought her for $200. Three weeks later Ebony Aztec came in season, so Elfriede, who never did get that mower, had her mated to a dog called Ungwilla Lad. That union produced Bavarian Aztec, who earned her compassionate owner $10,000 when she won the 1980 Vic Peters Classic final at Harold Park. Ebony Aztec became a great producer, with another of her offspring, Black Aztec, winning the 1980 Melbourne Cup, 1981 Australian Cup and $35,000 in prizemoney. He was later sold for $250,000 to a breeder in the United States, where he became one of the leading sires.

Another bargain success story was Kawati Boy, bought for $100 by a Canberra telephone linesman named Kevin de Smet. Kawati Boy won nine of his 15 races in 1978 and was named NSW Greyhound of the Year. Miss High Lo, the 1974 NSW Greyhound of the Year, who earned $46,000 prizemoney, also cost just $100 as a pup.

Jerry and Pat West, from the Sydney suburb of Belfield, in 1976 paid $350 for a dog called Top Replica, buying him out of the *Daily Telegraph* classifieds — hardly the place one would normally turn to for a potential star racer. Top Replica did not turn out to be a champion, but in January 1977 at Richmond, he ripped $20,000 off the bookmakers when he landed a well-executed betting plunge organised by his connections.

And in December 1970 a Sydney Water Board worker named Dave James paid just $50 for a dog called Alray Lad. Five months later, on 10 April 1971, Alray Lad won the Harold Park Bi-Annual Classic, one of the major races on the greyhound racing calendar. A decade later Ruth and Matthew Matic pulled the right rein when they took two puppies in lieu of $100 cash payment from a friend. One of the pups turned out to be World Park Ned, who gave the Matics their biggest win when he took out the 1983 National Derby final at Wentworth Park.

Then there is the story of Suemax, a crippled puppy who was a gift to Kevin Johns in 1979. Because of her disabilities Suemax could not be used for racing, but she became the mother of Manly Lion, Supreme Dot and Lord Buttons, who won $70,000 prizemoney for the railway linesman who only wanted to give their mother a good home.

Like all sports where money is involved, the greyhounds have had their share of scandals. Even so, I'll debate anyone, anywhere and any time on why they are most reliable betting medium. But more of that in another chapter where I'll tell the punters among you what to look for at the greyhounds.

A classic illustration of how little skullduggery there really is came in May 1982, when Jim Darcy, at the time the sport's biggest punter, had two dogs in the same race at Harold Park. World Rocket, trained by a fellow called Tommy Knott, and World Whizzer, trained by Ray Bruderlin, were litter brothers. Bookmakers opened World Rocket a 5/2 favourite with World Whizzer next in the betting at 7/2. When betting opened, Darcy told me: 'This is incredible. World Rocket has never been able to get within four lengths of World Whizzer when they have trialled together.' Accordingly, Darcy plonked massively on World Whizzer, who firmed to start a raging-hot 7/4 favourite, with World Rocket easing to 9/2. Unbelievably, World Rocket led all the way, beating his faster brother by two lengths.

My favourite long-priced betting story concerns a bitch called Lorna at Last, who was owned and trained in the late 1970s by Ron Bovis, a very good trainer from Albury. Bovis entered Lorna at Last for the nation's biggest race of that era, the Australian Cup, in those days run at the now-defunct Olympic Park track in Melbourne. He knew she was not really up to Australian Cup class, but he also knew she was going a lot better than her form indicated. Bovis posted away his entry form, hoping that Lorna At Least would draw one of the weaker heats. Sure enough, she came up in a race he was sure she could win, so he began putting a bank together. The bookmakers bet as much as 100/1 about Lorna at Last, with Bovis putting a cool $1000 on her. He averaged 66/1 for every dollar, showing a $66,000 profit when Lorna at Last scored an upset win. The bookmakers could pay out only part of Bovis' winnings, so the Albury trainer had to return the following week to collect the rest of his cash. Lorna at Last was no champion, but she set her battling bush trainer up for life.

Most greyhounds have a preference for a certain type of track. Some race better on roomy, horseshoe-shaped courses, others prefer tighter circuits with plenty of corners. The most unusual I've seen was Top Silhouette, who was a champ in the daylight but a chump at night. A regular competitor at Saturday afternoon meetings at Moss Vale and Goulburn, Top Silhouette was a champion at those tracks in 1970, winning a dozen races. But frustratingly for her owner she wouldn't produce her best form at Harold or Wentworth Parks, where there was big prizemoney, because they were night venues. Top Silhouette finally did manage to win a race in the city. When daylight saving was introduced she managed to get drawn in the first race one night at Harold Park and, running in almost daylight conditions at 7.30 pm, won easily.

The most successful trainer of all time was arguably Charlie 'Chicka' Morris, who is credited with training 6000 winners between 1931 and 1971. In the 1930s, '40s and '50s Morris would load up a caravan with dogs and travel around Australia, often winning four or five races at a country day meeting and repeating the performance at another venue that night. His most consistent dog was Fawn Mac, who won 18 races in a row at mechanical lure and what were called speed coursing meetings. Melbourne's White City and Maribyrnong tracks had no mechanical lure, but instead set a greyhound off after a live hare. The actual race field would then be released behind that first dog, which was called a pacemaker and was not part of the actual race. It was there simply to encourage the field to pursue the hare.

One of the best-known trainers of more recent times is Paul Cauchi, a Maltese migrant now in semi-retirement on Queensland's Gold Coast. Cauchi arrived in Australia in 1952 as a penniless 16-year-old. Although there was no greyhound racing in his native Malta, he became fascinated with the sport through attending race meetings here with friends. In the mid-1950s when he leased two dogs he was told one was good, the other a dud. Unfortunately for the kid from Malta, the good one died of hepatitis. But he managed to win eight provincial races with the other dog, Roy's Ace, who even got within a head of winning a race at Harold Park when sent out at the juicy odds of 50/1. Cauchi trained his first city winner, Gwydir Work, in May 1958, and saved enough money working as a gardener, construction worker and meat delivery man to buy and operate greyhound trial tracks at Toongabbie and later, in 1966, at Kellyville. Cauchi became as dominant in greyhound racing during the 1960s, '70s and early '80s as Gai Waterhouse is in thoroughbred racing today.

In October 1984 Cauchi left Australia to help set up greyhound racing in Santo Domingo, the capital of the Dominican Republic. Maurie Chippindale, a Sydney businessman, and three American partners, had been given permission by the Dominican government to build a track. Chippindale persuaded Cauchi to head to Central America to coach local employees on the art of training. But no sooner did Chippindale, Cauchi and the Americans have the sport on the verge of taking off than a change of government outlawed gambling on the dogs. The setback almost bankrupted the businessmen, and Cauchi returned to Sydney.

We'd all love to be able to back a prolific winner in a maiden race, but — and here's another one for Ripley's — that happened legally on two occasions in the 1970s.

A bitch called Killanahan, the fastest greyhound under live-hare coursing conditions in Ireland in 1972 and 1973, was imported for breeding purposes by well-known Melbourne racehorse and greyhound owner Charles 'Buck' Buchanan. After Killanahan arrived, Buchanan realised that under our rules, a greyhound was deemed to be a maiden if it had not won a race behind the mechanical lure.

Because all Killanahan's Irish wins had been chasing live hares, she was eligible to take on maiden puppies in a maiden race. In 1974 the wily Buchanan took her to Wyong, NSW, and duly landed a huge betting plunge with Killanahan, who had no trouble trouncing her inexperienced rivals.

Similarly, three years later, the champion hurdle dog Fiesta Ben was able to compete in a maiden race on the flat. Again, a loophole in the rules allowed him to start because, although he was Australia's best hurdler, Fiesta Ben had not won a flat race behind the tin hare. He had no trouble blitzing his rivals in a maiden event at Bathurst in June 1977.

Greyhound trainers tend to be battlers and the dogs have long been called the poor man's racehorses. But some of the owners and trainers have a great sense of humour. A bush trainer once brought a dog to a city meeting that was found to be covered with fleas. When the stewards remonstrated with the rough 'n' tumble trainer, they asked him if he realised his dog's condition. 'Too right,' came the reply, 'and tonight them fleas are gonna get the fastest ride they've ever had.' They did. The dog won.

Early in 2005 an owner and trainer named Frank Hurst had won 13 provincial races with a bitch called Rush of Gold. Despite this, Rush of Gold had not managed to win in 10 races at Wentworth Park, the Sydney track paying the big prizemoney. When another trainer mentioned to Hurst that his bitch did not seem to go as well at Wenty as she did on the country circuits, Hurst, noted for his dry humour, replied: 'I know. She hates racing on tracks where her owner gets $3200 first prizemoney.' Rush of Gold broke through for her initial city win at Wentworth Park on 8 January.

The biggest crowd I've seen in my 40-odd years covering the dogs was 16,300 at Harold Park in February 1970, but that attendance seems minuscule next to the 25,618 who turned up to watch greyhounds, ridden by monkeys, competing in hurdle races at Shepherds Bush track, now Mascot, in 1928. The monkeys, which were on loan from a travelling circus, were strapped onto the greyhounds. As recently as August 1970, officials of the Juarez track in Mexico repeated the gimmick, importing tiny Capuchin monkeys from South America to ride greyhounds in races.

17

The Secret World of Wine

There are always intriguing 'believe it or not' stories attached to greyhound racing, but the wine industry also yields its fair share of fascinating tales. Murray Tyrrell once told me how he discovered that the best Hunter Valley semillons are produced in wet vintages.

The finest Hunter semillons, which are invariably low in alcohol (under 11 per cent) and which see no oak, are unique to the world of wine and are acclaimed internationally. Yet according to Murray, in the 'early days' (pre-1960) the winemakers picked the grapes too late.

'We didn't know about preservatives, there was no refrigeration in the winery and we didn't have temperature-controlled storage cellars,' he told me. 'So the grapes were picked when they were very ripe. But because they were fermented in open vats they oxidised rapidly. Until 1960 most of the semillons made in the Hunter had more in common with sherry than dry white table wine. Then winemakers like Ray Kidd, Karl Stockhausen and Gerry Sissingh decided that chilling the fruit would be a big help. So we started throwing ice into the open vats. Of course if we overdid it completely the flavour would be diluted. But by being a little bit over the top with the ice we found, by accident, that the ice had lowered the alcohol. That reduction in alcohol seemed to suit Hunter semillon perfectly. The 1965, '67 and '68 Hunter semillons made in this way were exemplary. And that's when I realised that rain during vintage, which might be terrible for some grape varieties in other areas, would result in fantastic semillon in the Hunter.'

Incidentally, those great unwooded Hunter whites of the 1960s were not branded as semillons. In a classic example of cultural cringe, they were labelled as Hunter River white burgundy or Hunter River chablis, in awe as we apparently were of those great white-wine regions of France. Not only does Australia make unique dry whites like Hunter semillon, but we also produce another rare style, red wine with bubbles.

Opinions are divided as to the origin of what was formerly known as sparkling burgundy and now tends to be named after the grape variety used and labelled sparkling shiraz or sparkling cabernet. For 50 years Seppelt was the market leader of this style, and Ian McKenzie, their long-time chief winemaker, reckons the idea developed in France's Burgundy in 1918.

According to Macka there was a shortage of Champagne after World War I, so a resourceful Burgundian named Jacques Laussere decided to 'put bubbles into his red wines'. That notion eventually found its way here, but Australians embraced the concept with far greater zeal than French consumers.

However, veteran Barossa Valley winemaker Colin Glaetzer disagrees. He reckons Australian soldiers returning from France after World War I brought the sparkling red idea home with them, albeit by accident. Says Glaetzer: 'The Champagne region at that time produced a very good still red called Bouzy, and our soldiers were besotted by it. When they got back to Australia they asked a winemaker here to duplicate it. Because they said they had discovered it in the Champagne district, the Australian winemaker assumed it must have been bubbly. So he made a sparkling red. That's how it came about. And that's where the word "booze" comes from too. It was coined by those same World War I diggers, who originally were referring to that still red wine called Bouzy.'

Ian McKenzie incidentally used to relate a wonderful, no doubt apocryphal tale about the time the famous singer Dame Nellie

Melba visited the Seppelt underground sparkling wine caves in central western Victoria's Great Western district. 'Dame Nellie was the honoured guest and told her hosts that she had always dreamed of bathing in Champagne, as Australian sparkling wine was called at the time,' Macka told me. Anxious to accommodate her, the story goes that the Seppelt people filled a bath in the adjacent guest cottage with 60 bottles of bubbly. After Dame Nellie finished her bath, her hosts decided to re-fill the expensive bottles. Only this time, they discovered they seemed to have enough for 61 bottles.'

Although Europe's wine history obviously predates Australia's, we can lay claim to having the world's oldest shiraz vines. They are to be found at Tahbilk, in central Victoria's Goulburn Valley. The first shiraz vines were planted there in 1860, and Alister Purbrick, 51, now the fourth generation of his family to be winemaker there, is certain there are none in the world as ancient.

Purbrick points out that phylloxera, the bug which destroys grapevines, decimated the aged vines of France's Rhone Valley in the mid-19th century. 'These were not re-established until between

1880 and 1900,' says Purbrick. 'Similarly, Tahbilk is believed to be home to the world's oldest plantings of another Rhone Valley variety, the rare white grape marsanne. We planted marsanne at Tahbilk in 1927 and when leading Rhone Valley vignerons Monsieurs Chapoutier and Guigal visited us a few years back they conceded theirs dated only to 1930.'

It really is surprising that the world took so long to discover Australian wine. The current export boom — in the year ended January 2005, our overseas sales were 649 million litres worth $2.76 billion — did not begin until the mid-1980s. That was when Jacob's Creek, a brand first sold in 1976, propelled the 'brand Australia' name onto the world wine stage.

Our exports increased twenty-fold between 1984 and 1988 and by another 50 per cent by 2000. That Jacob's Creek now sells over five million dozen bottles a year, 80 per cent of which are exported to 65 countries, would have come as no surprise to the great American writer Mark Twain. Travelling the world in the 1890s, Twain visited the same underground cellars at the Great Western vineyards, near Stawell, central Victoria, that were later so favoured by Dame Nellie Melba. Twain wrote: 'The champagne, claret and hock I found matched the gold being discovered in the area. I saw 120,000 bottles of champagne kept in a maze of underground passages cut in the rock to secure it at an even temperature for its three years of maturation.'

The underground drives of Great Western, now owned by Southcorp, were dug by goldminers in 1885 and these days are home to over a million bottles of sparkling (what Twain mistakenly referred to as 'champagne') wine.

But it wasn't just overseas wine drinkers who were slow to discover our vinous treasures. Don Ditter, a former chief wine-maker for Penfolds, recalls that at the 1956 Melbourne Olympic Games the only reds available for sale were Cawarra Claret and St Cora Burgundy from Lindemans and from Seppelt either a Moyston or Chalambar Claret. When it came to whites the selection was even more limited, with Games visitors being able to choose only between Quelltaler Hock and Hamilton's Ewell Moselle.

And the four litre wine cask or 'bag in the box' was not invented until wine producer David Wynn and David Malpas, an engineer from Geelong, perfected the package in 1971. Earlier attempts, in 1966 by the Angove family and by Penfolds in the late 1960s, failed because the casks eventually leaked. Wine casks now account for 50 per cent of Australia's wine sales.

The Tyrrell and Drayton families are the backbone of the trendy, much-visited Hunter Valley area. Max Drayton, now 74, says his great-grandfather Joseph planted his first vineyard in the Hunter in 1857, five years after migrating from England. He made his first wine in 1860, while Edward Tyrrell, current chief executive officer Bruce Tyrrell's great-grandfather, produced his first vintage in 1864.

Although the Tyrrell and Drayton families are now household names in wine, the two family companies did not begin bottling their own wines until the early 1960s. Until then they sold their wines in bulk, with nothing being labelled. Says Max Drayton: 'Port, muscat and dry sherry were big movers at the cellar door and I remember people bringing in two-gallon demijohns to have them filled direct from our wooden casks. Our biggest customers though were Penfolds, Lindemans and McWilliam's, along with Leo Buring, who had a big wine shop in Sydney. Leo Buring used to catch the train to Cessnock and my brother Les, who had a taxi, would pick him up at the station and bring him to the winery.'

Similarly Murray Tyrrell made hundreds of wines which were bottled by great producers such as Maurice O'Shea of McWilliam's. All that changed in 1962 when a youthful Len Evans, at the time the beverage manager of the Chevron Hotel at Kings Cross, took a trip to the Hunter to bolster his hotel's wine supplies. Evans tasted the Tyrrells range and immediately persuaded Murray to begin bottling his wines under the family name.

Australia has a long wine history. Mary Laurie, who from 1876 to 1896 ran her family's winery on SA's Fleurieu Peninsula, less than 100 kilometres from Adelaide, was our first female winemaker. Maurice O'Shea, who studied viticulture in France in 1921, began making wine of an unprecedented high quality when he returned to Australia to become winemaker at Mount Pleasant, in the NSW Hunter Valley. In 1932 the McWilliam family bought into Mount Pleasant, and now produce some of Australia's finest semillons and shirazes there.

And the legendary Max Schubert, who joined Penfolds as a 16-year-old messenger boy in 1931, began making what is now the southern hemisphere's greatest wine, Grange, in 1951. Schubert, who had gone to Europe in 1949, principally to study sherry production in Spain, returned to Australia exhilarated about our potential to recreate the red wines of the Medoc district of France's Bordeaux region. While in the Medoc, Schubert had tasted 70-year-old reds which he discovered were made from predominantly cabernet sauvignon grapes and which had been matured in small 220-litre French oak barrels, rather than the 500-litre puncheon casks which were popular here.

When Schubert returned he could not source sufficient cabernet sauvignon to duplicate these reds of Bordeaux, so used shiraz, prolific here, in tandem with 220-litre barrels, and the Grange dynasty was born. After making Grange from 1951 to 1955, Schubert was instructed by Penfolds' board of directors to cease. One expert told him it tasted like port. Undeterred, Schubert continued to make the wine in secret, and by 1958 his wine was not only accepted but was being acclaimed as one of Australia's greatest tipples.

England's *Decanter* magazine acknowledged Schubert's efforts by naming him Man of the Year in 1988. I was privileged to meet Max in my early days as a wine writer, and was struck by just how modest and unassuming he was. Despite the fact that he was, by the late 1960s, a world wine legend, he eschewed elitism and had little time for wine snobs. I once delighted him with the story of how, when my wife was overseas, I heated up a frozen Big Ben meat pie and washed it down with a bottle of Grange. 'I can't cook but while I wasn't going to eat too well while Catherine was away, I was determined to still drink in a pretty flash manner,' I told him. The idea of somebody enjoying his famous wine with a good old Aussie meat pie thrilled Max.

18

Greyhound Racing's Champions

In 2004 greyhound racing celebrated the fortieth year of its most celebrated prize, the NSW Greyhound of the Year award. The judging panel comprises greyhound racing writers and broadcasters and I'm privileged to have been on every panel since the National Coursing Association launched the contest in 1965. In the *Daily Telegraph* in February 2005 I ranked my top 10 winners so far. For the record, they were, in my order of merit: Zoom Top, Rapid Journey, Tenthill Doll, National Lass, Winifred Bale, Miss High Lo, Worth Doing, Jessica Casey and the joint winners in 1966, Rose Moss and Roman Earl.

Over the years the judges' decision, which is made by secret ballot, has aroused plenty of controversy. So the final verdict comes down to a majority decision by the panel, and while there are parameters to guide us, ultimately we each select the greyhound we believe to have been the best of the year.

On occasion trainers or racegoers have claimed that a point-score system would make the award more accurate and less reliant on the opinion of the critics. But that just wouldn't work. Many years back in Victoria they had a point-score system operating for a similar award and the powers that be were mortified at the end of the year to discover the winning greyhound was a hurdler!

Hurdle racing is rarely conducted anywhere in Australia now, but in those days Victoria was the stronghold for hurdling, usually a last resort for dogs which weren't good enough to make it on the flat. The hurdler which won the Victorian dog of the year award had been racing virtually the same handful of rivals each week, and through the points method had amassed a greater tally than any of his vastly superior flat racing contemporaries. Not surprisingly, the Victorians ditched the point-score scheme forthwith.

But although there is no tangible cash prize or even a valuable trophy for winning the NSW award, a victory adds immense value to a male greyhound's stud value and also to the worth of the puppies produced by a female winner. Accordingly, feelings run very strongly, with the trainers of most finalists — these days there are three each year — believing their pooch deserves the crown. While who voted for which dog is not disclosed, I've never made a secret of my choice. That has sometimes caused a bit of consternation, and once it almost cost me a friend.

Back in 1971 the two standouts were Tara Flash, a wonderful sprinter-stayer, and the sport's undisputed sprint king, Pied Rebel. Paul Cauchi, a good pal of mine, trained Pied Rebel. I voted for Tara Flash, believing the remarkable versatility she displayed in winning over the two sprint distances and the two staying distances at the city tracks, Wentworth Park and Harold Park, gave her the edge.

When the result was announced in Tara Flash's favour, Paul was crestfallen. He later asked me how I voted and was stunned when I told him I had plumped for Tara Flash. 'I thought you were a mate of mine,' Paul said. When I replied that the award was for the greyhound of the year, not the mate of the year, he turned and walked away. He hardly spoke to me for about a week but came around when I explained my reason for giving Tara Flash the nod. And of course I added: 'Paul, I could have told you I voted for Pied Rebel and you would never have known the difference. But that's not the way I do things and I believe our friendship is a bit stronger than hinging on how I vote in a greyhound contest.' We were soon best of friends again.

I'm glad that was the case because a month later I was about to depart from Cessnock dogs when I discovered I had a flat tyre. As

I didn't have a jack in my car I panicked because the last race was well and truly over and the place was almost deserted. In the distance I noticed Paul Cauchi, who was invariably last to arrive and last to leave any greyhound meeting, about to get into his car.

I rushed over and asked if I could borrow his jack. Paul's travelling companion this night was a heavily built Maltese guy I only ever knew as Ringo, who was a big punter. Ringo asked me what type of car I had and when I replied it was a Torana he told Paul not to bother bringing the jack over. To my astonishment, Ringo, who was more rotund than Arnold Schwarzenegger-like in build, lifted the car up by the back suspension. I began working feverishly with the wheel brace but he told me there was no hurry. 'These cars are pretty light so take your time,' he said. Sure enough, Ringo had no trouble holding the Torana up in the air for the five minutes or so it took me to change the wheel.

Ringo was a funny guy. He often asked me for a tip but if the dog I suggested he back was any longer than around 5/1 ($6 in current terminology) he was loath to back it. He loved a favourite. Ringo was more confident if I tipped him a dog which was a hotpot and would simply invest more money. He hated backing outsiders.

But even Ringo would have baulked at taking odds of 17/1-on about a dog. That happened at Wentworth Park on Monday, 14 March 2005. That day there were non-TAB heats of the VIP Kennels Magic Maiden, each year's biggest maiden event run at the Glebe track. A Victorian dog called Atomic Jet was considered a shoo-in for the final, so when he drew box one in a field of four in the first heat, the bookies were not prepared to take any chances.

The dog was made a 17/1-on favourite but that didn't deter one punter, an ex-bookie named Peter Vanderfield. Fearless Pete put $1000 on Atomic Jet in a bid to win just $60. Things didn't look too good for the first 470 of the 520-metre race when a dog called Our Nemesis easily led the raging hotpot. Luckily for Peter, Our Nemesis tired badly over the last 50 metres and Atomic Jet got up to win. Peter risked $1000 to win $60, the hallmark of a true gambler. And I reckon he must have gone into the Guinness Book of Records in the process.

I've always numbered Peter Vanderfield among the most enthusiastic gamblers I've encountered. Between 1975 and 1984 he took a 10-year sabbatical, checking out cities where bookmakers operated around the world. Although most punters have long believed bookies can be found only in Australia, England and Ireland, Peter found them at Ostend, Belgium, and in Austria, Rome, Zimbabwe, Nairobi, Pakistan and India.

But the most unusual setting in which he discovered bookies was at a hound trailing meeting in England's Lakes District. 'Here the hounds followed a scent through the hills,' says Peter. 'On average there were 40 hounds per race, with each event taking around 45 minutes to complete. Betting continued during the running of the race and even though the dogs had no rugs to identify them, and were as far as two kilometres away, most people seemed to know who was winning. There were 13 bookmakers operating on the hound trailing fixture, so the betting was hardly of a token nature.'

Richard Zammit, now the president of the National Coursing Association and on the board of Racingcorp, owned National Lass, the 1984 and '85 award winner. I count him among my closest friends but in '84 I voted for his greyhound's arch rival, Turbo Top. This time though, I was in the minority, and National Lass won the title. These days Richard and I often share a meal and a bottle or three of good wine, and he usually gives me a good-natured rev up about voting against his favourite greyhound.

Greyhounds arouse passionate attachments among their owners and trainers to a far greater degree than racehorses or pacers. There are a couple of reasons for this. Greyhounds are dogs, after all, and among the many breeds of man's best friend there are few that are more affectionate and intelligent. Also, most horse owners have their animals trained by a professional and only get to see and pat their charges from a distance on race day, or once a week at the stables. But the average greyhound is a family pet Monday to Friday and races on a Saturday. That's why, as a journalist, I've learned to be very circumspect about what I write about individual greyhounds. There's an old saying that goes something like this: 'You can say what you like about an owner's wife or kids but don't bag his greyhound.' Suggesting that a greyhound has not chased keenly or, worse, has fought during a race will almost certainly earn you the owner's wrath.

John Carruthers, who with wife Jane owned and trained the sport's highest stake winning dog, Rapid Journey, has a great story along these lines.

'We got Rapid Journey through me taking a liking to a puppy that had been bred by George and Claudia Allen, greyhound breeders who lived near us,' says John. 'I asked George to put a price on him and from memory it was between $2000 and $3000, not cheap for a puppy in those days. But I really liked this youngster and as he was well bred I told George I would buy him. I nearly fell over when he replied to the effect that it wasn't as simple as that.

'George explained that before I could buy the pup I would have to come over to his place and have a cup of tea with him and his wife. According to George, if Claudia didn't like the look of somebody there was no way she would sell them one of her precious babies, no matter how expensive they were. I could hardly believe it. After all, I wasn't asking to take out their daughter, I just wanted to buy a greyhound puppy from them. But that was the situation so Jane and I had to meet Claudia before we could seal the deal. She must have approved because we got the pup, which we named Amerigo Magic. He was a smart race dog but when he finished racing and was mated to a bitch called Miss Courtney, who was owned by Jane's mother, the union produced Rapid Journey.'

Rapid Journey went on to earn $530,000 prizemoney for Jane and John Carruthers, who live on the western outskirts of Sydney. Their dog, now a family pet, served stints at stud in Australia and Ireland and remains the greatest prizemoney earner in the southern hemisphere. The kind of love people like Claudia Allen show for their greyhounds is typical and is a major reason why the dogs are the safest form of gambling. Most owners love their dogs so much they would never pull their pooch up. They'd be too frightened it might do the dog some harm. And these days, with prizemoney so good, there is far more incentive for an owner to win a race than to lose it. Few of the sport's participants even bet at all now, they race for the prizemoney and the thrill of winning.

When James Perry, who had a thoroughbred racing background, was appointed NSW's chief greyhound racing steward in 2003, I cheekily told him he had landed an easy job. 'What makes you say that?' James replied. I explained that at Wentworth Park, the state's major track, the average race was worth between $3200 and $3800 to the winner. 'The non-triers are gone,' I assured James. 'If I owned a hot favourite for a race and approached a bookmaker with an offer to pull the dog up if he paid me the equivalent of first prizemoney, he would laugh at me. These days the four or five bookies at Wentworth Park seldom hold $3000 on an entire eight-dog field so they certainly don't have much chance of getting more than that amount out of betting against one that can't win.'

James saw the logic of my argument and nodded, saying: 'That's a very good point.' In fact I can't remember the last time an owner or trainer was disqualified for pulling up a dog. And with sophisticated drug testing now in vogue, even go-fast dope like caffeine or cocaine is easily detected. I'm a keen punter so am the first to blow up if I think there is any skullduggery. But the sport has never been cleaner and I'm never afraid to have a bet on the dish-lickers.

19

How to Back Winners at the Dogs

I can't imagine writing about and tipping horses, dogs or trotters, and not having a bet. Yet I've seen racing writers, not many mind you, who weren't interested in having a wager. As a rookie reporter in the early 1960s I was astounded to see Fred Imber, then a racing writer with the Sydney *Sun*, sitting in the press room reading *Time* magazine during the pre-race action in the betting ring. I'm not saying Fred was not a good racing writer, but to me it seemed to be just a job to him.

Tipping greyhounds is not like being a carpenter or a butcher. One has to get really involved to do it properly. An old mate of mine, Norm Stapley, who is a keen punter, often blows up if a dog runs poorly, and shouts: 'All trainers should be forced to bet!' Norm's gripe is that many trainers these days send their dogs around in race after race, chasing the prizemoney but not really setting their charges for races the way the top trainers did in the 1950s, 1960s and 1970s. He reckons they would be more careful how they presented their dogs at the track if they were putting their cash on them.

Accordingly, I've always been a keen punter. But back in 1984, when my wife and I had two sons, Catherine was desperately trying to whelp a girl. She got some hotshot book on the subject which put us both on a certain diet, but more importantly, gave explicit instructions as to when it was most opportune to have sex. I recall heading off to Gosford dogs one night and as I left, Catherine sang out: 'Make sure you wake me up when you get back. According to my book it's the perfect time of the month for conceiving a girl so we have to do it tonight.' I replied: 'Well don't expect me to do the deed if I lose something like $3000. If I have a blackout at Gosford I won't even be able to get an erection. Having a root will be the last thing on my mind.' I can't remember if I won that night but perhaps I did, because around nine months later our daughter Sophie was born.

At the same time, most trainers don't know when their dogs are going to win. That's the truth. It's not that they don't know how their own dogs are going, but they are seldom capable of lining up the form of their opponents. I often have trainers approach me before a race asking me how I think their dogs will fare. A dog might have recorded a very fast time in a trial before a certain race, but may have box five. Its trainer is rarely aware of the traits of the dogs in the adjoining boxes, something crucial to greyhound races which are over in between 20 and 44 seconds.

A few years back a friend of mine rushed to the press room at Wentworth Park breathlessly informing me that a dog in box eight, prepared by Sydney's leading trainer, was a certainty. The trainer had told my mate that his dog had clocked the fastest time ever run on his home trial track. I took the wind out of my mate's sails when I told him I considered the dog a 100/1 chance. 'It has box eight and wants box one, it's not a flash beginner, and the dogs in boxes six and seven are wide runners. It'll be a miracle if it doesn't get knocked down early.' And that's what happened. You see, the trainer concerned knew what his dog could do, but like most trainers had not watched countless video replays of races, the way professional tipsters, punters and bookmakers do. So, generally speaking, trainers are not acquainted with the mettle of their opposition.

One of the best judges I've encountered among trainers is Alan Chauncy, who trained former top-class stayers Mockacindy and Chief Mocka and who sold the champion sprinter Woolley

Wilson as a pup. Alan is now in semi-retirement in Queensland, pottering around with a few dogs as a hobby. He was one trainer who usually knew what his rivals were capable of, simply because he was an enthusiastic punter. Sometimes he would tip me one of his greyhounds, adding: 'She is beautifully drawn in box one because I backed the dog in box two at its last start and it is the widest runner I've seen.'

Incidentally, Alan once told me the story of how Gary Wilson, a crippled and partially blind lad who became the subject of an especially moving episode of *This Is Your Life*, came to secure Woolley Wilson.

On the TV show Gary said he had gone to Chauncy's kennels to select a pup from a litter. 'I sat at the end of the yard and declared that the first pup to come up to me would be the one I'd buy,' Gary told the show's host, Roger Climpson. 'Next minute this little puppy with a fluffy, woolly coat was in my lap so I took him home with me.' It was a lovely romantic yarn because Woolley Wilson, trained by Geoff Watt, became the champion sprinter of his time.

But Alan put another slant on the tale when he told me: 'I thought I'd be able to sell all the pups from this litter I had except maybe this funny-looking little thing with the woolly coat. So when Gary announced that the first pup to come to him would be his pick, I put my foot under the woolly-coated dog and punted him into Gary's lap. That's the true story.' Gary of course had the last laugh, as Woolley Wilson was easily the best in the litter.

So what should one look for to find a winner at the dogs? For my money the most important single factor is the box draw. The box draw at the dogs is far more crucial than the barrier draw at the horses or even at the trots. The average punter assumes box one is the best but that's not necessarily so. A dog which is a wide runner, especially if it is a slow beginner, is probably badly off in box one. Most wide runners are better placed in box seven or eight, the two outside traps. But that's not to say a wide runner can't win from box one. If it is positioned on the rails, and the dogs in boxes two and three are also wide runners, the greyhound in box one is likely to get a good cover from the other pair in the charge to the vital first bend. Similarly, a so-called crasher — a dog which veers sharply towards the inside rail when the boxes open — is nearly always hard pressed to win from box seven or eight. But if the crasher is a fast beginner and the dogs drawn inside him are slow starters, he or she may be able to cross to the rails without suffering interference and be in front at the first turn.

This is why knowing as much as possible about the habits and racing traits of every dog is a big help in backing winners. By the time every Wentworth Park meeting is over I endeavour to have a detailed comment written alongside every dog which has raced that night. This is done through watching the replays of each event seven or eight times. Maybe one of the dogs involved is trained at, say, Broken Hill, and may not race again in Sydney for six months. But when it does return I can refer to the comment I entered when it previously raced in the city, thereby having some idea about the dog's peculiarities. The beauty of greyhound racing is the dogs run spontaneously. Accordingly, if a greyhound is a fast beginner, nine times out of 10 it will be up near the lead at the start. If it is an established slow starter, chances are it will be at the back of the pack going to the first turn. Ditto for good railers and wide runners.

With horse racing a keen punter may work out a race on the premise that a horse will make the pace. But the jockey may have different ideas and decide to ride the horse from behind the lead, thereby throwing the punter's calculations out the window. That simply can't happen at the dogs. Because they chase by instinct, greyhounds simply get out and go like hell when the starting boxes open. It's that spontaneity that makes the longtails the most attractive betting medium.

The so-called 'squeeze' boxes — four and five — once wryly known on country tracks as the 'visitors' boxes' (meaning they were supposed to be allotted to dogs from out of town) are usually, but not always, the worst draws. Again it comes down to the attributes of the dogs drawn in these positions. A brilliant beginner in box four may have no trouble going straight to the front if the dogs in boxes one, two and three are notoriously slow starters. Even a slow beginner but very good railer in box four may have a good chance of finding a good rails run at the first bend if the dogs in one, two and three are extremely wide runners.

Early speed therefore is crucial, and these days nearly every track displays sectional times after each event. At Wentworth Park these signify what the pacemaker — not necessarily the winner, of course — ran to the first and second marks. Keen punters record these sectional splits in an endeavour to ascertain the likely leader in future races.

Many punters swear by racing weights but I'm not one of them. Unlike at the horses or trots, greyhounds are weighed when they are brought to the racetrack. Unless a greyhound weighs within one kilogram of its previous racing weight it is scratched by officials. That's good enough for me, but some punters will shy away from a dog because it is down .4 of a kilogram or up .6 of a kilogram from its previous racing weight. Of course a variation of .4 of a kilogram on a 36-kilogram dog means far less than it does on a little 23-kilogram bitch.

Years ago I followed weights, but soon found that small discrepancies turned me off too many ultimate winners. By all means take note of racing weights, but remember that they have more relevance in long-distance than short-course races and are less likely to affect the performance of a large dog than a small bitch.

In England, where six- rather than eight-dog fields are the norm, the railers are placed in the inside boxes and the wide runners on the outside. If a trainer registers his dog as a railer and there are three railers drawn in a particular race, the draw is conducted for boxes one, two and three. Ditto for the wide runners in the same event. While the English system makes for relatively interference-free racing, it also produces a plethora of short-priced favourites and results in boring racing. Since most Australian trainers don't bet, they'd like to see the UK method implemented. That's because their dogs would suffer less inter-ference and possibly sustain fewer injuries. But betting turnover would fall dramatically due to a prevalence of odds-on chances stifling betting. Then prizemoney would tumble.

And the UK scheme takes away the glorious uncertainty of the sport. I still get a terrific buzz from successfully working out how a race is going to be run. Because greyhounds run spontaneously, times are obviously important. But they can be misleading too. On many race cards, the best dogs don't clock the fastest times. A smart fourth-grade dog, getting its own way in front and leading throughout, will often run a quicker time than the winner of the top-grade race on the same program. Yet when that same fourth-grader is elevated in class, it is often incapable of reproducing its previous slick time. This is because in top-grade races there are several greyhounds of equal ability, all capable of running similar times. There can be more jostling for the lead in top-grade races than in low-grade events where one dog is able to assert its superiority quickly. That's why, when I'm punting, I prefer to bet in weak low-grade events than the feature races. It is easier to back the winner of a fifth-grade race at Wentworth Park than it is to land the victor in the Golden Easter Egg final at the same course.

After the box draw, I consider the class of race next in importance. It is amazing how often a dog which has been losing in third-grade races can bounce back to the winner's circle when it is dropped to fourth-class. It's just like a footballer who doesn't shine in first-grade looking like a superstar when he goes down to reserve-grade. Put it this way: I would sooner back the class dog in a race than the one with the fastest winning time.

Generally speaking, it is better to back a dog that has good early speed but is not strong at the finish, than to put your cash on a slow starter who is powerful at the end of its races. A weak leader can often pinch a race through the dogs behind it collid-ing, thus enabling it to get away with a huge break. The only time slow starters come into their own is when scratchings reduce fields from eight to six or seven runners. It's amazing how one or two less than the usual number of starters in a race can allow slow beginners to be closer to the lead than they are in complete fields of eight.

The greatest blight on greyhound racing are dogs which don't chase the mechanical lure keenly. Unfortunately there are more of them now than there were 40 years ago. In the 1960s stewards tended to only drug-test greyhounds which staged a form reversal. A dog which won on Saturday but ran poorly on Monday would be tested, as would a greyhound showing a sudden form improvement. Accordingly, if a trainer had a dog which was not a keen chaser, he could give the dog a hit of caffeine a couple of hours before it raced. That usually made the dog try harder, and the trainer was relatively safe from incurring the ire of the stewards so long as his dog raced consistently. So the trainer would give the suspect chaser a dash of caffeine every time it raced.

These days, with greyhound racing, like all sports, required to be totally drug free, there is no place for bad chasers or fighters. If a dog is deemed to have failed to pursue the lure keenly or to have fought (in reality such dogs are not fighting, but playing with another dog) it is banned for a month from the track on which it offends. A second offence leads to a three-month suspension from all tracks and a third conviction ends the dog's career. Assisted by video replays of races, modern-day stewards move quickly to ban dogs which are blatant non-chasers.

But greyhounds which just run a lot of second placings are harder to catch. Keen punters are able to recognise dogs which tend to chase the leading greyhound rather than the lure. There are plenty of greyhounds which are reluctant to go past the leading dog, but will run like the wind to reach it. Avoid these greyhounds when betting on a win basis but keep them in mind for the exotic forms of betting such as trifectas (naming the first three placegetters in correct order) or exactas (first and second in finishing order).

My favourite betting form of the so-called exotics is the trifecta. Trifectas can sometimes pay extraordinarily well, simply because no approximate dividends are displayed before each race. If a dog (or a horse for that matter) is paying win odds of 10/1 on the TAB and is only 4/1 with the bookies, sharp-eyed trackside punters will back the dog via the course totalisator and so destroy the off-course bettor's chances of a dividend windfall. But that can't happen with trifecta betting as there are too many combinations for approximate dividends to be displayed.

The best way of tackling trifectas is to select the two best chances. If I like numbers two and six, I'll take two to win, six to run second and the rest of the field for third. Then I'll also take six, two, field, and, in case of a split, two, field, six and finally, six, field, two. To cover each of those combinations for the minimum bet of a dollar, costs, in an eight-dog race, a total of $24. I've had some nice wins by this method, especially when the outsider in a field combination has finished second, splitting my two fancied runners. In such instances a divvy of $100 or more is not uncommon.

20

Kamahl Puts a Wine Writer
to the Test

When I began writing about wine, like most newspaper wine critics, I had no formal wine-tasting training. A couple of wine journos, such as Queensland's Peter Scudamore-Smith, have passed the rigorous Master of Wine examination, but most have become reasonably adept at assessing wine simply through years of practice. And rating wine is a bit like judging movies or books. Beauty is in the eye of the beholder.

I might love a certain movie or book and recommend it to a friend only to be told it was disappointing. Wine drinkers are probably best advised to find a critic who has similar tastes and stick with that critic's judgment. I'm an enthusiastic fan of rhythm 'n' blues music and a couple of decades ago subscribed to a British magazine called *Blues and Soul*. I eventually sorted out one reviewer whose taste was so in sync with mine that I bought any album he praised sight — or rather, hearing — unseen. I was never disappointed.

Long before I began writing about wine I was tasting it, buying it, reading about it and visiting areas where it was made. Whenever I backed a winner at the dogs I'd head out to Farmer Brothers' bottle shop at Wellington Street, Waterloo. Then I'd fill the car boot with reds and whites from around the world, and although my budget didn't extend to the most expensive Bordeaux and Burgundies from France, we were getting seven francs to the dollar at the time, as opposed to around four francs now. So I was able to taste a wide range of French wines from regions like Alsace and the Rhone and Loire valleys.

Like most critics, who have had no formal wine-tasting training, consumers can also become skilled at appraising wines. Basically if your health is good — that is, if your sense of smell has not been impaired and your tastebuds are in order — you can evaluate a bottle of wine. My advice is: don't be intimidated or daunted, because if you can taste food, you can rate wine. It's only a matter of practice.

Don't take my word for it. That advice comes from no less a source than Andrew Caillard, a Master of Wine and the brains — or should I say the palate — behind the successful Langton's Wine Auctions.

Says Caillard: 'Wine industry lore about people having good and bad palates is nonsense. There are educated palates belonging to people who do nothing else but taste wine for a living. But anyone who has a sense of smell and can taste different flavours can assess wine.'

John Fordham, wine writer for the *SundayTelegraph*, once told me of a dinner party at the home of the popular singer Kamahl, a family friend. 'When I arrived,' said Fordham, 'Kamahl pulled out a bottle of sparkling wine wrapped in brown paper. He wanted me to taste it and tell the gathering what it was. I feared I was about to be humiliated in front of all these people when I remembered that the new Brian Croser-made sparkling wine had been released that day. I also knew that Kamahl was friendly with the people who distributed the Croser wine, so I thought there was a good chance he had been sent some samples. So I took a punt, sniffing and sipping and then said that while the wine had Champagne-like characters, it was unmistakably Australian, not French. I declared it was probably the new Croser. Everyone applauded and Kamahl declared me a genius.

'But I wasn't off the hook yet. Before we sat down to dinner Kamahl dashed inside and came back with another brown paper-encased bottle of bubbly. As I was tasting it, Kamahl's teenage son came up behind him and held up a hastily written sign which revealed the wine's name. From past experience I knew Kamahl's son loved to play tricks on his father so I cheekily told Kamahl, "That's easy. It's Mumm Cordon Rouge non-vintage from Champagne." Of course everyone was now in on the joke except Kamahl, who threw his hands in the air and said: "No wonder you're a famous wine writer, I can't stump you at all. Now let's eat dinner." I breathed a massive sigh of relief.'

When you open a bottle of wine the odds are that if it looks fine, with a bright appearance, and a pleasant smell, it is going to taste good. Young reds should be purple to ruby red, before becoming reddish brown with a few years bottle age and then developing a mahogany or amber brown colour when fully mature. White wines begin life the palest of yellow, sometimes with a slight green tinge around the rim of the glass when poured. With age they go from mid-golden yellow to a deep golden, brownish yellow and when they are over the hill become a light brown colour.

At shows wines are given points out of 20 and are awarded a maximum of three for colour, seven for bouquet and 10 for taste. Once in the glass a wine should not have a cloudy or even dull appearance. But suspended matter, especially in an old red, is no cause for alarm. Wines like this usually only need decanting. The easiest way is to pour the wine through a tea strainer into a jug, then back into the bottle again via the tea strainer.

However, alarm bells should ring with a wine that has a mouldy odour or reeks of wet cardboard. It is probably corked, which has nothing to do with bits of cork floating on the wine's surface. A corked wine has been spoiled through a faulty cork or, in a less likely scenario, tainted oak barrels. Either way you should not, and are not expected to, accept such a wine. But you can't send a bottle back simply because you don't like the taste.

A few years back a sub-editor at the *Daily Telegraph* told me he had a raging argument in his local bottle shop when he tried to return a bottle of aged Hunter semillon. The sub-editor insisted it was off, while the bottle shop owner, almost certainly correctly, was adamant that was how the wine was supposed to taste. Old semillons and rieslings develop a deep golden colour and a toasty aroma that often comes with petrol or kerosene-like characters. Wine buffs acclaim these wines but the average punter finds them offputting. It turned out my sub-editor friend had never drunk a five-year-old white before and simply hated the taste. Finally his retailer refunded him the cost of the bottle, adopting a 'customer is always right' approach. But I advised my workmate to stick with one- or two-year-old whites in future.

Of course a genuinely faulty wine should be returned to the bottle shop or restaurant. Don't be bashful about returning such a bottle — but don't drink it first. If the wine is indeed corked the supplier will be given a credit for the offending bottle by the distributor. People sometimes ask me about those little flakes occasionally found floating in white wines. These are tartaric acid crystals and are completely harmless. They don't affect a wine's flavour and certainly won't make you ill.

So-called experts often talk about a wine's balance. All that means is they have found each of its components in harmony. That is, there is no excess of tannin, acid or oak. Tannin is that mouth-puckering, sometimes astringent sensation one gets from red wine. It is a by-product of oak, along with grape skins and seeds. The body of wine refers to its weight. An oaked chardonnay will almost certainly be heavier than an unwooded version and a shiraz more robust than a merlot or a pinot noir.

The hallmark of a good wine is a long finish. Such a wine shows longer-than-usual retention of its taste in one's mouth after swallowing. It denotes quality in both red and white wines.

When it comes to serving wine, whites should not be over-chilled and reds should not be served at 'room temperature' on a hot summer's day in Sydney. The 'room temperature' rule for serving reds originated in Europe and certainly doesn't apply to a searing February day in Sydney.

My biggest wine stuff-up occurred when my in-laws Robert and Marcelline Vivien came to Australia in 1974 for the marriage of their daughter Catherine. Anxious to show off Australian wine to my future father-in-law, a French wine enthusiast, I pulled the cork on an old bottle of Penfolds Grange I had been cellaring for several years. We were about to enjoy an outdoor January lunch and I was full of expectation as I poured Robert his first taste of Grange. I watched in horror as he took a sip, jumped up and headed into the house, returning with his glass of Grange bolstered with a couple of ice cubes. I thought it was the act of a philistine to chill such a classic, expensive wine, but to Robert's taste it was now much more palatable.

Of course it was my error. Grange was not the wine to be serving at an al fresco summer barbecue anyhow, but by the time Robert got his first taste it was even less suitable, close to being luke warm. When served too warm, a red wine's fruit is swamped by the alcohol.

According to Phil Laffer, chief winemaker for Orlando Wyndham, we not only serve our reds too warm, but our whites too cold. 'A long spell in a refrigerator will see a white come out at around four degrees and that is just too cold,' says Laffer. 'At that temperature you might as well be drinking water with a dash of alcohol because you won't pick up the wine's intrinsic flavours. But it can be worse. I was once in Helsinki for a tasting and even though it was minus six degrees they served the whites direct from the fridge! I reckon 15 degrees is a good ambient temperature, although really good Champagne can be chilled down to eight degrees, but no colder. Of course it's all relative. If it is very hot outside you can drop the wine temperature by a couple of degrees.

'Conversely, reds should not be served warmer than 18 degrees. Plonking a couple of ice cubes into a glass of red won't hurt the wine at all. All that a bit of water does to wine is it dilutes the acidity. It won't affect flavour or bouquet.'

Richard Rowe, chief winemaker for WA's Evans and Tate, reckons white wines should be served at different temperatures, depending on the style. 'I would serve chardonnay at between eight and 10 degrees but aromatic whites like sauvignon blanc and riesling can do with a bit more chilling,' says Rowe. 'But if you are drinking any of them outdoors on a summer's day in Sydney you can serve them pretty cold because the glasses will soon heat up.'

According to Canberra's best-known winemaker, Ken Helm, a good rule of thumb is to serve cheap whites icy cold but better-quality bottles lightly chilled. 'That's because drinking a white at near freezing temperature will hide its faults,' says Helm. 'I serve whites at around seven degrees and reds at slightly lower than body temperature, rules which I find reveal all the aromatic sensations of wine.'

What about fortified wines such as tawny and vintage ports or those terrific liqueur muscats and tokays from north-east Victoria? These are invariably consumed at room temperature but Dean Kraehenbuhl, who made Penfolds Grandfather Port, one of our most famous fortifieds, for a couple of decades, reckons that is wrong.

In summer, Kraehenbuhl pops the glasses which are to be used for fortified wines into the freezer section of the fridge for 10 minutes. 'You can also serve fortifieds over some crushed ice because they should not be served warmer than 17 or 18 degrees,' Kraehenbuhl has always said.

I've picked up a couple of handy wine serving and storing hints over the years. To chill a wine at short notice, place the bottle for 30 minutes or so in an ice bucket containing equal amounts of ice and water. And if you have a cellar, and want to prevent bugs eating away the labels, give the front of each bottle a protective coating with a squirt of cheap hairspray.

Not too many people cellar wines these days. In fact wine company research shows around 85 per cent of all wines purchased are consumed within 48 hours. But if you do want to put away some good-quality reds or age-worthy whites such as Hunter Valley semillon or riesling from the Clare or Eden valley, you don't need an expensive, elaborate cellar.

The main thing to remember is that to age well, wines need to be housed in a constant temperature, somewhere between 10 and 18 degrees. At a higher level than this, wines will mature too quickly. Also avoid excessive light. If this can't be easily achieved, wrap your bottles in newspaper.

Wines under cork, as opposed to the current fad of being screw-capped, should be stored on their sides to keep corks moist. A dry cork will contract, admit air, and eventually cause the wine to oxidise. If you cut an apple or a banana and allow it stand for a few minutes, it will turn brown (oxidise). The same thing happens with wine, which, after all, is made from fruit.

Dampness should be shunned too, although some humidity helps keep corks pliable and resilient. A container of wet sand kept within the cellaring area will promote the right amount of moisture. Suitable bottle storage containers include agricultural pipes, racks made of steel or wood, slats held up by bricks, polystyrene boxes or even cardboard banana cases. These can be placed in a garden shed, providing it is insulated and has good tree cover, a fireplace with a bricked-up chimney, or under the house or staircase. But don't store wine in cupboards above a stove or fridge, next to a water heater or in an enclosed shed alongside lawnmower fuel and garden chemicals.

Good drinking!

21

How I Struck the Lottery

I feel a bit like A.B. Facey must have when he wrote that marvellous memoir *A Fortunate Life*, although I haven't done it anywhere near as tough as Mr Facey. But I certainly have been extremely fortunate to have spent over 40 years — so far — enjoying every minute of my working life. After all, greyhound racing and wine are, apart from my wife and kids, my two consuming passions, and not many people get to combine work with one, let alone two, of their great loves.

Not only that, I grew up within a wonderful family and then by a freakish fluke — fate I guess — I found Catherine in Paris and married her. Lionel Rankins, a great old Runyonesque character who used to put the *Daily Mirror* formguide pages together in the 1970s and 1980s, thought the world of Catherine. He used to tell me, in his own inimitable fashion: 'Pigeon, you're so lucky to have found her I reckon you could put your hand down the shithouse and come up with a gold watch and chain.'

Fate is a funny thing. I often wonder what would have happened if I had not been able to back a few winners and so afford that trip to watch the rugby league World Cup in 1972. Or if I hadn't noticed the Paris phone number scrawled on one of the newspapers Buck Buchanan gave me to read on the trip to Europe.

I've also been lucky to have been writing about wine during that industry's most prosperous era. In 2004 France sold 8.2

million dozen bottles to the United States, yet the family-owned Yellow Tail brand from the NSW Riverina managed US sales of 7 million cases on its own during the same 12-month period.

Yellow Tail is the most amazing among a swag of feel-good success stories in wine. In June 2005, the 20 millionth case of Yellow Tail left Australian shores, bound for Japan. Although the first Yellow Tail wine was not blended until August 2000, the company's merlot and shiraz were America's biggest sellers within four years. Perhaps even more remarkable, a mere two decades earlier the Casella family, owners of Yellow Tail, were not even selling their wines to bottle shops. They only sold them to friends.

The Yellow Tail saga began when Maria and Filippo Casella emigrated from Sicily in the late 1950s and through picking grapes in the Riverina and cutting cane in north Queensland were able, in 1965, to buy a small farm at Yenda, near Griffith, NSW. The farm happened to contain some grapevines and four years later the Casellas were making a small amount of wine which they offered to friends. Most of their customers were mates they had made in the Queensland cane-cutting industry. So Filippo would regularly put his available wine stocks into old wooden beer barrels, stack them onto his truck, and drive from Yenda to far north Queensland selling his booze. Incredibly, considering Yellow Tail's worldwide success, they did business that way until 1990.

Although most people enjoy a glass of wine these days, many don't know how it is made. Nobody describes the process more succinctly than Phil Ryan, the acclaimed multi-award-winning winemaker for McWilliam's Mount Pleasant Winery in the Hunter Valley.

Says Phil: 'After the grapes are picked they go into a roller crusher, which is like an old-fashioned washing machine wringer with fingers attached to remove the stalks. The stalks are sucked into a pipe while the rest, called the must, runs into the sump at the bottom. The must, comprising juice, seeds, skins and pulp, is then separated. White grape juice has to be chilled while it is fermenting but this isn't the case with reds. We do control red fermentation though because if it gets too hot some flavour is lost. White juice is separated from the skins with drainers and a day later the skins are transferred into tank presses. With reds, we put the lot, minus the stalks, into fermentation tanks and a couple of weeks later the wine is put into tank presses. Next we remove the wine and press the skins again, repeating the process to get maximum value from the grapes. Tank presses have something like an air bag inside. The skins are dropped out, the bag fills with air and gently squeezes out the juice. Next the wine is filtered before going into wood to mature. Most wines benefit from maturation in oak although we use stainless steel for aromatic white varieties like semillon, riesling and traminer.'

Phil Ryan is typical of the 'salt of the earth' characters who make up the Australian wine industry. After all, winemakers are basically farmers. They just happen to harvest grapes rather than wheat or rice. Not for them the elitism or snobbery which still exists among some wine consumers. A classic example of this was described to me by a McWilliam's colleague of Ryan's who visited China on an export venture. There he saw Chinese businessmen drinking Chateau Petrus, a French red which costs $1000 a bottle, mixed 50/50 with lemonade or cola. They obviously did not like the taste of the famous Petrus, but felt it was 'right' to be seen with a few bottles on their table!

Most of the greyhound industry people I've met are very much like those in the wine trade, really down-to-earth folk with a 'what you see is what you get' manner about them. While the wine industry is flourishing, thanks to our healthy exports, now worth around $2.76 billion annually, greyhound racing is struggling to attract new participants.

In NSW the sport accounts for 18 per cent of betting turnover and is the fastest growing, bets-wise, of the three racing codes. But these days most of the fans watch the racing from their loungerooms. And who can blame them? They can have a betting account with the TAB or a bookmaker operating at the track and watch the races broadcast live on Sky Channel.

But I believe syndications are the answer to get the fans back to the track. A good greyhound, ready to race and capable of winning in the metropolitan area, can be purchased for $10,000 to $15,000. And training fees are minuscule compared to thoroughbreds, which cost around $70 per day to be with a professional stable. Most greyhound trainers charge only a nominal fee of something like $50 a week in return for 50 per cent of the dog's earnings on the track. This is a great system because it encourages the trainer to place the dog where it can win prizemoney and keeps expenses down for the owners.

I often get calls from acquaintances keen to form greyhound-owning syndicates but who are in the dark as to how to go about finding the right dog or trainer. When greyhound racing's official-dom finally gets around to organising brochures detailing how to form such syndicates, through which a group of friends can have a lot of fun, with their own racer, for just a few dollars a week, the sport could be on the way back to its glory days.

Off-course betting and telecasting means we will never again see 16,300 people attend a greyhound meeting, as they did at a Harold Park meeting in February 1970, but I'm certain there are prosperous times around the corner. I look forward to still be writing about them, just as I have been privileged to be around during the wine boom.